CW01652307

THE ZOO BOOK OF LAUGHS

ZOO

Published by Carlton Books Limited 2007
20 Mortimer Street
London W1T 3JW

Text and photographs copyright © 2007 EMAP
Design and layout © 2007 Carlton Publishing Group

This book is sold subject to the condition that it shall not, by way of trade or otherwise, be lent, resold, hired out or otherwise circulated without the publisher's prior written consent in any form of cover or binding other than that in which it is published and without a similar condition including this condition, being imposed upon the subsequent purchaser. All rights reserved.

ISBN 978-1-86200-518-1

Printed in Great Britain

ZOO MAGAZINE
Editor: Ben Todd
Editor-At-Large: Michael Hogan
Designer: Steve Dobson
Coordinator: Clair Terry

THE ZOO BOOK OF LAUGHS

SEVENOAKS

CONTE

NTS

ZOO EDITOR'S LETTER

Welcome to *ZOO*'s great big *Book of Laughs*!

We all know that *ZOO* is the greatest mag on this earth – so we thought we'd put together a book for you. Just because we really are very nice.

Whether you're a) on the bus b) on the loo c) or just plain bored of listening to the girlfriend waffling on about romantic comedies/mortgages/*Desperate Housewives*/engagement rings/her mother, we think we know exactly the way to cheer you up – make you laugh.

So we've brought together our most hilarious jokes, our first class quotes and those just piss-your-pants funny bits that keep us giggling throughout the year.

And we've put them in one amazingly good value book, which is now in your hands.

This, *ZOO* have scientifically proven, will keep you grinning . . . whatever the girlfriend insists on rabbiting on about. True.

It's that simple.

The ZOO Book of Laughs is here to make you titter, snigger or just pass out with amusement . . . for literally hours!

So welcome, one and all, you are now officially part of the world's greatest magazine.

That doesn't mean you automatically get to bed Scarlett Johansson, Keeley Hazell, Jessica Alba or all three at once – but it does make you a happier person. Trust us.

Ben Todd

Editor, *ZOO*

ZOO FOOTBALL

"You know, I always thought football was a bit gay."

SLY STALLONE, WHO ODDLY WASN'T BRAVE ENOUGH TO SAY IT ON A TRIP TO GOODISON PARK

"WHY WOULD I WANT TO GIVE EVERY PENNY I'VE EARNED TO SOME HORRIBLE LITTLE CHAV FOOTBALLER SO HE CAN BUY HIS WIFE DRESSES TO WEAR AT AINTREE? I'D RATHER PISS IT UP THE WALL."

NOEL GALLAGHER RULES HIMSELF OUT OF BUYING MAN CITY

"I THINK I LOOK VERY ATTRACTIVE."

WAYNE "DENIAL" ROONEY ON THE COCA-COLA POSTER OF HIM AND COLEEN

"In my past ten games I've scored ten goals. Could I be any better?"

No, not Cristiano Ronaldo. It's Marek Saganowski. Of Southampton

"NINETY MINUTES BEFORE A GAME THERE IS NOT MUCH A COACH CAN DO. YOU CAN'T TALK TO PLAYERS, SO YOU SIT DRINKING TEA."

Former England boss Sven-Goran Eriksson neatly sums up his five-year reign

"He's tall/He's mad/He dances like your dad/Peter Crouch/ Peter Crouch."

Favoured chant from England fans

"WAYNE ROONEY IS LIKE ME, BOTH AS A PLAYER AND A PERSON. HE COMES FROM A ROUGH AREA AND I LIKE THAT."

Diego Maradona sees a little of himself in England's golden boy

"It didn't take that robotic dance to make Peter Crouch look freaky – he already looks like a terminally ill child crossed with a flamingo."

Frankie Boyle

"I did not have any nerves, although I did go to the toilet just before I came on so there might have been some there." THEO WALCOTT REVEALS HIS ARSENAL DEBUT PREPARATIONS

"He's Greek/He's great/He'll smash your dinner plates/Samaras, Samaras!"

Man City fans to striker Georgios Samaras

"Are you shagging Elton John?"

NEWCASTLE FANS TO THE WATFORD END

"Are you shagging Ant 'n' Dec?"

THE WATFORD SUPPORTERS RESPOND

"We need to score from midfield. I told the players 'Frankie Lampard's got 17'. They just said 'Perhaps that's why he's on 150-odd grand a week'."

PORTSMOUTH BOSS HARRY REDKNAPP GETS A REALITY CHECK

"TEVEZ FOR STAR TREK!

***Villa fans chant to West Ham's alien-faced signing*"**

"I watch a lot more football these days than when I was younger. I never really went to games then, as I was playing."

SHAUN WRIGHT-PHILIPS LOOKS ON THE BRIGHT SIDE OF LIFE ON THE SUBSTITUTES BENCH

"Rooney was protesting and complaining all the time. Wah wah wah. He reminded me of my kids"

Horacio Elizondo, the referee who sent off Wazza in the 2006 World Cup England vs Portugal quarter-final

"We were able to test ourselves against better players. And the showers were warm – we're not used to that."

Yeading skipper Nevin Saroya speaking after losing 5–0 to Nottingham Forest in the FA Cup

"Sir David Beckham? You're having a laugh. He's just a good footballer with a famous bird."

PLYMOUTH BOSS IAN HOLLOWAY ISN'T IMPRESSED BY TALK OF A KNIGHTHOOD FOR DAVID BECKHAM

"Football is football and everyone sniffs around everyone else's back door."

STUART PEARCE LETS SLIP WHAT HAPPENS IN THE MAN CITY SHOWERS

"What the national coaches are doing is like taking a car from your garage without asking permission. They then use the car for ten days and abandon it in a field without any petrol left in the tank. We then have to recover it, but it is broken down."

ARSENAL BOSS ARSENE WENGER, WHOSE 1ST XI COMPRISES INTERNATIONAL PLAYERS, KNOWS THE FEELING

"WE PASSED LIKE SHIPS IN THE NIGHT. HE WAS A HUGE RICH YACHT AND I WAS A LITTLE ROWING BOAT."

Graeme le Saux on leaving Chelsea just as Roman Abramovich arrived

"PEOPLE ARE ENTITLED TO THEIR OPINION. NOT THAT I'LL EVER WATCH *WITHOUT A TRACE* AGAIN."

Former Sydney FC Coach Terry Butcher on actor and shareholder Anthony LaPaglia's call for his head

"If you're a superstar and earn more than anybody else, you have to lead from the front. They didn't. At times they behaved like shits."

Danish International Thomas Gravesen on his time at Real Madrid

CLASSIC GAZZA GAGS...

When asked to mouth his own name for the BBC's Italia 90 coverage, Gazza chose to mouth "Fucking wanker" instead – which the Beeb duly used for the rest of the tournament.

He booked a course of sun-bed sessions for Tony Cunningham, his Newcastle team mate.
Tony Cunningham is black.

On the eve of a match against Norway, a Norwegian tv crew asked Gazza if he had a message forhis opponents.
"Fuck off Norway!" he replied, before running off.

Told the president of the Danish FA that he could speak Danish, before doing his best *Muppet Show* chef impression.

On his first night in Rome after joining Lazio, Gazza got away from his minder, left his shoes by an empty window and hid in a cupboard. The poor minder was convinced his charge had killed himself jumping out the window...

"According to recent Government figures, in the last three years 600,000 immigrants have come to England to seek work – half of them in the Premiership."

Dara O Brian – Mock The Week

"I have to answer the phone a lot more and I'm no good at that. I have a face for radio without the voice. I've also got to find a matchday suit that fits me."

Bolton boss Sammy Lee ponders his job

"WAYNE ROONEY IS A BULL, SO STRONG HE'D BE PERFECT FOR ANY JOB. INCLUDING HELPING YOU MOVE HOUSE."

Spain's Michel Salgado pays tribute

"I had a dream about Didier Drogba the other night. He's gorgeous. I came into work all distressed because it had gone wrong at the end."

GMTV's Fiona Phillips likes a big striker up top

"My God, it's like 'do you want to die or do you want to die?'"

Thierry Henry is asked to choose between never scoring again or never having sex again

"LOOK AT ME. I JUST SIT IN MY BROTHEL ALONE WATCHING TV. THE MEN AREN'T INTERESTED, THEY'RE ALL WET AND BEER-SODDEN. IT'S A CATASTROPHE."

German prostitute on how the 2006 World Cup has been bad for business

"I've prepared some new tricks, like something out of* The Matrix*."

Portugal's Cristiano Ronaldo bends over backwards for his country

"Players should masturbate consistently. It doesn't wear them out, is a major physical boost and stops them chasing skirt."

LEADING SEXOLOGIST GERMANICO ZAMBRANO ADVISING ECUADOR'S NATIONAL TEAM

"I can understand that people say I'm arrogant. I saw myself walking on the TV not so long ago and I thought to myself 'That's an unpleasant posture – can't I change the way I walk?'"

ARSENAL'S ROBIN VAN PERSIE DOES SOME SOUL-SEARCHING

"I praise my son for defending the family's honour and have nothing but contempt for Materazzi. I want his balls on a platter."

THE FURIOUS MOTHER OF ZINEDINE ZIDANE AFTER HIS 2006 WORLD CUP SHAME

"Maybe Big Sam's pushed Anelka's bed up against the wall so he can only get out on the good side."

PAUL MERSON ON NICOLAS ANELKA'S CONSISTENT FORM FOR BOLTON

"It's like Amsterdam. They look great in the window, but turn out to be dogs."

COMIC BOB MILLS ON THE PERILS OF THE TRANSFER WINDOW

"I got bombed. I made sure I was in the same team as the lads who aren't being picked, but I still think they were shooting at me."

ROY KEANE ON SUNDERLAND'S TEAM-BONDING PAINTBALL SESSION

"If it was a boxing match, it'd be Muhammad Ali against Jimmy Krankie."

AIDY BOOTHROYD ON WATFORD TAKING ON MAN UNITED

"Noel drags it out a little bit, but Deal Or No Deal *is still pretty good. I switch off once the big money boxes have gone, though."*

SO THAT'S HOW MICHAEL OWEN SPENDS HIS TIME WHEN HE'S INJURED

"HE ISN'T A ROBOT. SOMETIMES WE FORGET HE IS HUMAN."

Frank Rijkaard plays down Ronaldinho's killer instinct on the field

"Ryan could play football in a phone box and find the door, no matter how many players you put in there with him."

MAN UTD ASSISTANT COACH CARLOS QUEIROZ'S TRIBUTE TO RYAN GIGGS. ER, RIGHT

"Cristiano Ronaldo goes down too easy for my liking but remember, he's literally had two big men up his backside for 90 minutes."

Tony Gale goes into innuendo overload on Sky Sports

"WHAT A COMPLETE CHICKEN NUGGET WITH DOUBLE BARBECUE SAUCE HE IS."

PLYMOUTH BOSS IAN HOLLOWAY AFTER PAUL CONNOLLY IS INJURED

"I feel very determined and really hungry."

ONCE-FAT FOOTBALLER FRANK LAMPARD'S COMMENTS ABOUT HIS FOCUS ON THE PITCH GET MISCONSTRUED

ZOO SHOWBIZ

"The only thing I want to go on is Deal Or No Deal. *Not a special edition, the normal show. I'll be Simon from Barnsley, see if anyone notices."*

ARCTIC MONKEYS DRUMMER MATT HELDERS ON HIS MOST SHOWBIZ AMBITION

"Kinder Surprise chocolate eggs: must be bought separately rather than in packs, because it's more likely the toys inside are different."

HIGHLIGHT OF THE MOTORHEAD FRONTMAN LEMMY'S 35-PAGE BACKSTAGE RIDER

"I don't like watching myself. Telly makes me look a little overweight and actually I'm an incredibly slender man."

MATT LUCAS: GOOD SELF IMAGE

"I was thieving when I was about 11, before I became an arty c*. We'd run into a sweet shop, grab stuff and fuck off. I was a good little thief."**

Danny Dyer on his law-abiding childhood

"When I die, even if I've been knighted, it'll still be: Welsh Toilet Duck man quacks his last quack."

Rob Brydon fears being remembered more for voiceovers than his shows

"I've sponsored a child in Africa. She's got a Jimmy Carr t-shirt, a Jimmy Carr hat. But I worry if it's making any difference. I'm not getting any more bookings." **Jimmy Carr**

"If I saw an ugly bird but she was a celebrity with loads of money, she wouldn't attract me at all."

Rio Ferdinand on how star-shagging doesn't work in reverse

"STING IS ALWAYS BOASTING ABOUT EIGHT-HOUR SEX MARATHONS WITH HIS WIFE. IMAGINE HOW LONG HE'D BE ABLE TO GO IF SHE WAS A LOOKER."

Jimmy Carr

"Rik Waller is 60 per cent fat. That's the same as a pork scratching."

RICKY GERVAIS

"Glastonbury was very wet and muddy. There was trench foot, dysentery, peaches… all the Geldof daughters."

SEAN LOCKE, *8 OUT OF 10 CATS*

"Carol Vorderman is considered the thinking man's crumpet. Presumably by any man who's thinking 'I wouldn't mind shagging some mutton dressed as lamb tonight.'"

ANGUS DEAYTON, *WOULD I LIE TO YOU?*

"The staff in my local Waitrose are really blasé about me now. They'll be like, 'Him? Oh he's in here all the fucking time. And between me and you, he doesn't eat very well.'"

Noel Gallagher on grocery shopping

"That new Heineken ad slogan, 'Get the head right and the rest will follow.' Wasn't that Abi Titmuss's career plan?"

IAN HYLAND, *NEWS OF THE WORLD*

TOP TEN STRANGEST BACKSTAGE RIDER REQUESTS

1. Red Hot Chili Peppers

Meditation Room in medium to dark colour (preferably not blue) including coffee table and rug.

2. Whitney Houston

One coach and/or two 15-passenger vans, two mini-buses and/or two 15-passenger vans, Mercedes S-Class or 600 series or BMW 740. All vehicles MUST BE ARMOURED.

3. Marilyn Manson

Two bottles of Absinthe.

Four bags of Haribo Gold Gummi Bears. Must be Haribo Gold Bears.

4. Paul McCartney

A properly trained canine search team required to conduct a sweep of the stage and backstage area at 5pm.

"Nice and comfy" furniture in white or off-white – not any animal skin or print.

Six floor plants "that are just as full on the bottom as the top. No trees, please."

5. Ozzy Osbourne

Three oxygen tanks.

Ear, nose and throat doctor on site, able to administer a B12 and decadron (anti-inflammatory) shot.

6. Foo Fighters

Four pairs of white tube socks (US size 10–13).

Four men's boxer shorts (medium).

Four Kinder Eggs.

7. DMX

One gallon Hennessy Cognac.

Three boxes of condoms (Trojan, Lifestyle or Kimono's).

8. EMINEM

Two sofas.

One full-length mirror.

Soft toilet paper, Kleenex and fresh hand soap.

Game room including large TV with PlayStation and games, masseur, ping-pong table and portable basketball hoop.

9. ICE CUBE

36 KFC Hot Wings.

Four Bic lighters.

One copy of *USA Today.*

10. Black Eyed Peas

Professional, English-speaking, *sober* monitor engineer.

> *"Jennifer Aniston goes to Malibu to shout at the sea. I drink Malibu and shout at pigeons."*
>
> BILL BAILEY

"He's the least fashion-conscious person I've ever met. Coleen cuts his hair but if she's not about, his mum does it."

WAYNE ROONEY'S BIOGRAPHER HUNTER DAVIES

"I REALLY FANCY COLEEN. SHE'S SO SLUTTY. AM I A DIRTY OLD MAN?"

CHRIS MOYLES ADMITS TO "FEELINGS" FOR WAYNE ROONEY'S FIANCÉE

ALAN COCHRAN: *"I missed the entire Diana concert 'cos I went to the pub with some Diana lookalikes that haven't worked in 10 years. I just thought they needed cheering up."*

JIMMY CARR: *"Harry apologised to his troops for not being with them. I watched the gig and I would have rather been in Iraq."*

8 OUT OF 10 CATS

"I Googled myself this morning and got 7,333,600 matches. Everything from me being a god to the anti-christ. Hey, maybe I am the anti-christ."

DAVID HASSELHOFF HAS A SEARCH ENGINE-BASED IDENTITY CRISIS

"People often ask me what it was like working with Hollyoaks *girls. I say ' It was hard. In fact it was constantly hard for four years.'"*

FORMER SOAP "STAR" AND *LOVE ISLAND* RESIDENT LEE OTWAY

"Where do I see myself in 20 years? Looking like Noel Edmonds."

Justin Lee Collins

"I do charity work now. I get people off drugs. I used to get drugs off people."

RUSSELL BRAND

"What fragrance do I wear? Opium. The one by Yves Saint Laurent obviously."

PETE DOHERTY HEADS OFF THE HEROIN GAGS

"I demand a takeaway. I'm drunk and it's my right."

PEEP SHOW'S ROBERT WEBB AFTER A FEW ALES

"David Mitchell's like a walking David Attenborough documentary. He's got the eyes of a shark, the brain of a dolphin and the flight of a gazelle."

FRIDAY NIGHT PROJECT'S JUSTIN LEE COLLINS ON HIS POSH *PEEP SHOW* MATE

TOP TEN RAPPERS' REAL NAMES

1. *Method Man – Cliff Smith*
2. *Xzibit – Alvin Joyner*
3. *Ja Rule – Jeffery Atkins*
4. *Ludacris – Christopher Brian Bridges*
5. *Common – Lonnie Lynn Jr.*
6. *MC Hammer – Stanley Kirk Burrell*
7. *Ol' Dirty Bastard – Russell Jones*
8. *Ginuwine – Elgin Lumpkin*
9. *Ice T – Tracy Marrow*
10. *Snoop Doggy Dogg – Cordazer Calvin Broadus*

"Hello, I'm Jimmy Carr, I'm one of the biggest faces of British comedy. Literally."

Jimmy Carr

"P. Diddy throws the biggest, but mine are small and potent. I just invite the right people. I'm efficient with my parties."

Jamie Foxx. Maybe he's got no mates

"I MET A LITTLE GIRL WHO HAS CANCER BUT SHE'S, LIKE, BETTER NOW BECAUSE SHE GOT TO HANG OUT WITH ME. I'M SO GLAD I CAN TOUCH PEOPLE'S LIVES LIKE THAT."

PARIS HILTON HEALS THE WORLD

TOP TEN JOBS POP STARS DID BEFORE THEY WERE FAMOUS

1. **Noel Gallagher – baker.**
2. **Ronnie Vannucci (Killers) – wedding photographer.**
3. **Ricky Wilson (Kaiser Chiefs) – art teacher.**
4. **Fergie (Black Eyed Peas) – voice of Sally on Charlie Brown cartoons.**
5. **Nelly – scouted by Atlanta Braves and Pittsburgh pirates to play pro baseball.**
6. **Ice Cube – trainee architectural draftsman.**
7. **Kurt Cobain – janitor for Lemons Janitorial Services.**
8. **Coolio – fireman.**
9. **Jay-Z – sales clerk at Kennedy Fried Chicken.**
10. **Ozzy Osbourne – abbatoir worker.**

"There are rumours that Nicole Richie is pregnant. Apparently you can tell because she's only throwing up in the morning."

CRAIG FERGUSON, US TALKSHOW HOST

"We got to the checkout and there's this square thing, and I'm like what's this, guys? They said, 'That's so you can use your credit card'. I was like, 'You can use credit cards in grocery stores now?'"

Down-to-earth Janet Jackson visits a supermarket

"There's still a world full of people out there who think there's not much more to me than the girl who can wear tiny tops."

WE'VE NO IDEA WHAT JENNIFER LOVE HEWITT'S ON ABOUT, HAVE YOU?

"My tattoos are always free, man. I can pretty much walk in anywhere I fancy and they'll do one for free. If they're not, I'm walking out."

HEAVILY-INKED RAPPER THE GAME

"If I could change anything about myself, it'd be the heat levels in my body. I blush and people always think I fancy them. Actually I'm just really hot."

TV PRANKSTRESS DAISY DONOVAN FLUSHES WITH SUCCESS

"A cockroach can live for a whole week without a head. Beat that Heather Mills!"

Jimmy Carr

"Imagine being in the kitchen of the curry house next time Jade Goody goes in."

Dara O'Brian

"It's because my nether regions always hang to the left, like an aubergine."

GORDON RAMSAY ON WHY HE CALLED HIS FIRST RESTAURANT AUBERGINE

"All that matters in music today is that your song becomes a ringtone."

COLDPLAY'S CHRIS MARTIN HITS OUT AT RECORD LABELS

"I did a charity gig for cancer last week. If I ever get cancer, I'll be in the ward saying, 'See that machine? I paid for it. Now get that little bald fucker off it.'"

RICKY GERVAIS

"I still live like a student but with nicer carpets."

STEPHEN MERCHANT SUMS UP HIS POST-FAME LIFESTYLE

"My wife bought me a pedometer recently. You're meant to take 10,000 steps a day and I did 15,000, just lazing at home. I can't keep still. That's why I'm so thin."

Office-*turned*-Pirates of the Caribbean *star Mackenzie Crook: twitchy*

"I get so much attention for being sexual and beautiful, so I down-play that side of myself."

LOST STAR EVANGELINE LILLY. ANYONE ELSE JUST STOPPED FANCYING HER?

"I've had enough of spending £100 an hour on therapy sessions. I thought I might as well get a pair of trainers. It's the best therapy I've ever had. I wish somebody had told me that 12 years ago."

Ronnie O'Sullivan on the powers of shopping

"I've only ever bought one album – But Seriously *by Phil Collins. I was 15, decided to get into music, went into WH Smith and that was No1, so I assumed it was the best."*

David Mitchell from* Peep Show *on his paltry music collection

"Ms Spears did not vomit on him. He just had peanut butter on his hands."

BRITNEY'S PUBLICITY PEOPLE DENYING SHE PUKED ALL OVER A NEW MALE BEAU

"Sky News, a channel where people don't swear? Fuck that! Fucking nutbag! Oops, are we live? I do apologise. It was a joke."

Dame Helen Mirren turns the air blue on the Baftas red carpet

"I'm tired of the attention I'm getting from men. I can't go out without someone hitting on me."

JESSICA SIMPSON IS ALREADY TIRING OF THE SINGLE LIFE

"If I was invisible for the day, I'd go over to Bob Geldof's and slap Peaches."

The Friday Night Project*'s Alan Carr speaks sense*

"I'm not a bad person. I genuinely don't want to upset anybody. Off the air, I'm quiet, shy almost."

DJ CHRIS MOYLES INSISTS HE'S NOTHING LIKE HIS LOUDMOUTH, RADIO PERSONA

"Ricky Gervais tries to fuck you up. He'll fart in the middle of a scene and won't crack a smile."

Kate Winslet recalls her nun episode of *Extras*

ALL IN THE NAME

The three wise men arrived to visit the child lying in the manger. One of the wise men was exceptionally tall and smacked his head on a low beam as he entered the stable. "Jesus Christ!" he exclaimed.
"Write that down, Mary," said Joseph "It's better than Derek."
popbitch

FRIGHT NIGHT

Two nuns are driving down a road late at night when a vampire jumps onto the bonnet. The nun who is driving says to the other, "Quick! Show him your cross." So the other nun leans out of the window and shouts, "Get off our fucking car!"
Posted on the sun.co.uk

TAKING OFF

A guy sitting at a bar at Heathrow Terminal 3 noticed a really beautiful woman sitting next to him. He thought to himself: "Wow, she's so gorgeous she must be an off duty *flight attendant*. But which airline does she work for?" Hoping to pick her up, he leaned towards her and uttered the Delta slogan: "Love to fly and it shows?"

She gave him a blank, confused stare and he immediately thought to himself: "Damn, she doesn't work for Delta." A moment later, another slogan popped into his head. He leaned towards her again, "Something special in the air?" She gave him the same confused look. He mentally kicked himself, and scratched Singapore Airlines off the list.

Next he tried the Thai Airways slogan: "Smooth as Silk."

This time the woman turned on him, "What the fuck do you want?"
The man smiled, then slumped back in his chair, and said "Ahhhhh, Ryanair!"

TOUGH LOVE

What's the difference between your wife and your job?
After ten years your job still sucks.

DOPEY SHAG

The seven dwarfs went to the Vatican, and because they are 'THE DWARFS', they are ushered in to see the Pope.

Dopey leads the pack.

"Son," says the Pope, "What can I do for you?"

Dopey replies, "Excuse me, your Excellency, but are there any dwarf nuns in Rome?"

The Pope wrinkles his brow at the odd question, thinks for a moment and answers, "No, Dopey, there are no dwarf nuns in Rome."

In the background, a few of the dwarfs start giggling.

Dopey turns around and gives them a glare, silencing them.

Dopey turns back, "Your Worship, are there any dwarf nuns in all of Europe?"

The Pope, puzzled now, again thinks for a moment and then answers, "No, Dopey, there are no dwarf nuns in Europe."

This time, all the other dwarfs burst into laughter.

Once again, Dopey turns around and silences them with an angry glare.

Dopey turns back to the Pope and says, "Mr. Pope, are there ANY dwarf nuns anywhere in the world?"

"I'm sorry, my son, there are no dwarf nuns anywhere in the world."

The other dwarfs collapse into a heap, rolling and laughing, pounding the floor, tears rolling down their cheeks as they begin chanting:

"Dopey f***ed a penguin!... Dopey f***ed a penguin!"

JOKE'S ON YOU

Bloke answers the phone and it's a casualty doctor.
The doctor says,"Your wife was in a serious car accident, and I have bad news and good news. The bad news is, she's lost all use of both arms and both legs, and will need help eating and going to the bathroom for the rest of her life."

Bloke says,"My God. What's the good news?"

The doctor says,"I'm kidding. She's dead."

WHOLESOME STORY

An old lady dies and goes to heaven. She's chatting it up with St. Peter at the Pearly Gates when all of a sudden she hears the most awful, blood curdling screams.

"Don't worry about that," says St. Peter,"it's only someone having the holes put into her shoulder blades for wings."

The old lady looks a little uncomfortable but carries on with the conversation. Ten minutes later, there are more blood curdling screams."Oh my God," says the old lady,"now what's happening?"

"Not to worry," says St. Peter,"She's just having her head drilled to fit the halo."

"I can't do this," says the old lady,"I'm going to hell."

"You can't go there," says St. Peter."You'll be raped and sodomized."

"Maybe so," says the old lady,"but I've already got the holes for that."

CUT AND RUN

So I got a job as the Queen's hairdresser. I parked outside Buckingham Palace and a policeman said to me:"Have you got a permit?"

And I said "No – I've just got to take a bit off the back."

Tim Vine

Two fish swim into a concrete wall.
One turns to the other and says:"Dam!"

SHARE THE LOVE

"How many Jews does it take to screw in a lightbulb?
One, you anti-Semitic piece of shit."
Louis Ramey, stand-up

SCARY TALE

A TV reporter goes to a retirement home to interview an aged but legendary explorer. The reporter asked the old man to tell him the most frightening experience he had ever had. The old explorer didn't hesitate: "Once I was hunting Bengal tigers in the jungles of India. I was on a narrow path and my faithful native gun-bearer was behind me. Suddenly the largest tiger I've ever seen leaped onto the path in front of us. I turned to get my weapon only to find the native had fled. The tiger leapt toward me with a mighty ROARRRR! I soiled myself."

The reporter said, "Under those circumstances, sir, anyone would have done the same."

The old explorer replies, "No, not then – just now when I went ROARRRR!"

Comedy Central, US TV show

THE BACON TREE

Two Mexicans are stuck in the desert, wandering aimlessly and close to death. They are close to just lying down and waiting for the inevitable, when all of a sudden…

"Hey Pepe, do you smell what I smell. Ees bacon I is sure of eet."

"Si, Luis eet smells like bacon to meee."

So, with renewed strength, they struggle up the next sand dune, and there, in the distance, is a tree loaded with bacon. There's raw bacon, dripping with moisture, there's fried bacon, back bacon, double smoked bacon... every imaginable kind of cured pig meat.

"Pepe, Pepe, we is saved. Eees a bacon tree."

"Luis, are you sure ees not a meerage? We ees in the desert don't forget."

"Pepe when deed you ever hear of a meerage that smell like bacon... ees no meerage, ees a bacon tree".

And with that... Luis races towards the tree. He gets to within five metres, Pepe following closely behind, when all of a sudden, a machine gun opens up, and Luis is cut down in his tracks. It is clear he is mortally wounded but, a true friend that he is, he manages to warn Pepe with his dying breath.

"Pepe... go back man, you was right ees not a bacon tree."

"Luis Luis mi amigo... what ees it?"

"Pepe... ees not a bacon tree... Ees ... Eees a Ham Bush."

What do you call a woman who knows where her husband is every night?

A WIDOW

Why did the scientist fit his door with an old fashioned knocker?

HE WANTED TO WIN THE NO-BELL PRIZE

OLD FARTS

An old man and his wife have gone to bed. After lying there for a few minutes the old man farts and shouts, "goal!"

His wife rolls over and asks, "what in the world was that?"

The old man says, "Goal! I'm ahead 1–0."

A few minutes later the wife lets one go and shouts, "Goal! 1–1!"

After another ten minutes, the old man farts again. "Goal! 2–1!"

The wife quickly drops another and, starting to enjoy herself, shouts, "2–2!"

Not to be outdone, the old man strains as hard as he can to squeeze out the winning fart. Unfortunately, he tries too hard and shits the bed. The wife asks, "Now what in the world was that?"

"Half time," replies the old man. "Switch sides..."

WHAT DO YOU CALL A SCOTTISH CLOAKROOM ATTENDANT?

ANGUS MCCOATUP

Innkeeper: "The room is £15 a night. It's £5 if you make your own bed."

Guest: "I'll make my own bed."

Innkeeper: "Good. I'll get you some nails and wood."

HE'S ALL GIVE

Did you hear about Paul McCartney's lavish wedding presents for Heather?

He bought her a plane. And a Ladyshave for the other leg.

An elderly couple walk into a fast food restaurant. They order one hamburger, one order of fries and one drink.

The old man unwraps the plain hamburger and carefully cuts it in half. He places one half in front of his wife. He then carefully counts out the fries, dividing them into two piles and neatly places one pile in front of his wife. He takes a sip of the drink, his wife takes a sip and then sets the cup down between them. As he begins to eat his few bites of hamburger, the people around them keep looking over and whispering "That poor old couple - all they can afford is one meal for the two of them." As the man begins to eat his fries a young man comes to the table. He politely offers to buy another meal for the old couple. The old man replies that they're just fine - they're just used to sharing everything.

The surrounding people noticed the little old lady hadn't eaten a bite. She sits there watching her husband eat and occasionally taking turns sipping the drink.

Again the young man comes over and begs them to let him buy another meal for them.

This time the old woman says "No, thank you, we are used to sharing everything."

As the old man finishes and wipes his face neatly with the napkin, the young man again comes over to the little old lady who had yet to eat a single bite of food and asks "May I ask what is it you are waiting for?"

The old woman answers..."THE TEETH."

FIGHT CLUB

"For my birthday I got a humidifier and a de-humidifier. I put them in the same room and let them fight it out."

Steven Wright

Q: What do you call a little German who lives in a tin?
A: Heinz.

AN EYE FOR THE LADIES

Two men bump into each other in an airport. The first man says "I can't see my wife."

The second replies "What a coincidence, I can't find mine either. What does yours look like?"

First man: "She's 5ft10, blonde, big boobs, mini skirt, stockings, stilettos and a boob tube. What's yours look like?"

Second man says: "Never mind her, we'll look for yours."

Daily Star

FEELING SHEEPISH

A Carlisle fan is trapped on a remote desert island with a sheep and a dog. Soon, the sheep starts looking really attractive to the Carlisle fan. However, whenever he approaches a sheep the dog growls in a threatening manner.

The man takes the dog to the opposite side of the island, giving it some food as a distraction. He runs back to the sheep only to find the dog growling at him. The man ties the dog to a tree with a large leash. He goes back to the sheep only to find the dog growling with a gnawed-off leash around its neck.

By now, the man is getting depressed and frustrated. As he sits under a palm tree staring out to sea, a beautiful woman in a tight-fitting wet suit emerges from the surf.

She asks him who he is and, taking pity upon his lonely state, asks if there's *anything* she could do for him. The man thinks for a moment and then responds, "Could you take the dog for a walk?"

What has 90 balls and screws old ladies?

Bingo

What do you call someone who covers his genitals in chickpeas and garlic?

A hummusexual

popbitch.com

A man goes to the doctor and says, "Doctor, I've got a strawberry stuck up my arse." The doctor says, "I've got some cream for that."

LITTLE NOT LARGE

Little Johnny walked in one day on his daddy in the bathroom. He asked his father what that was hanging between his legs. His father replied that it was the perfect penis. The next day at school, Johnny pulled his pants down in front of his classmates.

"What's that?" asked Jenny.

"'Well," said Johnny, "if it was about three inches smaller, it would be the perfect penis."

A BIG DISAPPOINTMENT

A young couple leave the reception and arrive at the hotel where they're spending their wedding night. As the groom removes his socks, the bride says: "What's wrong with your feet? Your toes look all mangled and weird."

"I had tolio as a child," he replies.

"You mean polio?"

"No, tolio. It only affected my toes."

As he takes off his trousers, his new wife asks: "And what's wrong with your knees? They're all lumpy and deformed."

"As a child I also had kneasles," he replied.

"You mean measles?"

"No, kneasles. It only affected my knees."

He finally removes his y-fronts. "Don't tell me," she sighs. "Smallcox?"

Tam Cowan, Daily Record

WHAT A DRAG

Two men were changing in the locker room after a game of tennis. One notices the other one is putting on a pair of stockings and suspenders. He says "When did you start wearing them?" To which the other man replies "Since my wife found a pair on the back seat of the car."

Why does Mike Tyson cry during sex?
Mace will do that to you.

ANY EXCUSE

A guy calls his boss and says, "I can't come in for work today. I'm sick."
The boss said, "How sick are you?"
The guy says, "I'm f___ing my cat."

A bloke offered me a brand new widescreen telly. OK the volume knob was stuck on maximum, but then he only wanted a quid for it. I mean, how could I turn that down?
Tim Vine, stand-up

What do you call 100 nuns in a shop? Virgin Megastore

Q: Did you hear about the angry fly on the toilet seat?
A: He got pissed off.
popbitch.com

LITTLE RUN-AROUND

This morning on the way to work I rear-ended a car at some lights while not really paying attention. The driver got out and he was a dwarf. He said, "I'm not happy..."
I replied, "Well, which one are you then?"
popbitch.com

AY AY AY CAP'N

There once was a pirate captain who, whenever it looked like a battle would be imminent would change into a red shirt. After observing this behaviour for a few months, one of the crew members asked him what it meant.

"It's in case I get shot. I don't want my crew members to see blood and freak out."

"That's very sensible, sir." At that moment, the crew member spotted eight hostile ships on the horizon. The captain all of a sudden looked very concerned:

"Fetch my brown pants, bo'sun."

Q: How many gay men does it take to put in a lightbulb?
A: One. But it takes an entire A&E department to get it out.

b3ta.com

Q. What did the Mexican fireman name his two sons?
A. Jose and Hose.

popbitch.com

BROTHERS IN ARMS

What have Richard Hammond and Pete Doherty got in common?
They both do *Top Gear* and have had Moss on their face.

ISEE

Apple Computer announced today that it has developed a computer chip that can store and play music in a woman's breast implants. The iBreast will cost £499. It's considered to be a major breakthrough because women are always complaining about men staring at their breasts and not listening to them.
The Sun

A Frenchman, a German and a hypochondriac arrive at a hotel.
"I'm tired and thirsty", says the Frenchman. "I must have wine!"
"I'm tired and thirsty," says the German. "I must have beer!"
"I'm tired and thirsty," says the hypochondriac. "I must have diabetes."
The Guardian

In an interview about his failed marriage, Sir Paul McCartney was asked if he'd ever go down on one knee again. He replied: "I'd prefer it if you called her Heather."

Monica Lewinsky is looking in a mirror. Her frustration over her lack of ability to lose weight was depressing her. In an act of desperation, she decides to call on God for help. "God, if you take away my love handles, I'll devote my life to you," she prays.
And just like that, her ears fell off.

"How does Bob Marley like his doughnuts?
Wi' jammin'."
Peter Kay

YOUNG AT HEART

Did you know that Michael Jackson just turned 47?
Yeah, but he still feels like a 13-year-old sometimes.

"Did you hear about Vanessa Feltz getting arrested at customs?
She was trying to smuggle 40lb of crack in her knickers."

LEGS 11

What did Britney's right leg say to her left leg?
Nothing, they've never been seen together

Luke Skywalker and Obi-Wan Kenobi are in a Chinese restaurant and Luke's having trouble with his chopsticks.
Finally, Obi-Wan says, "Use the forks, Luke."

SAW IT COMING

A woman walks into Specsavers to return a pair of glasses that she'd purchased for her husband a week before.
The assistant says, "What seems to be the problem, madam?"
"I'm returning these glasses I bought for my husband", she says, "He's still not seeing things my way."
popbitch.com

SAW IT COMING

A chav girl goes to the doctors complaining of a weird green rash on her inner thighs. The doctor takes one look and says "Tell your boyfriend his gold earrings are fake."

Good news:
Pete Doherty has entered a 12-step programme.
Bad news:
he lives 12 steps from a crack house.

HOW MANY KIDS WITH ATTENTION DEFICIT DISORDER DOES IT TAKE TO CHANGE A LIGHTBULB?

WANNA GO BIKE-RIDING?

From the Bumper b3ta Book of Sick Jokes

Q: How many cool people does it take to screw in a light bulb?
A: What? You don't know?

Why does Dr Pepper come in a bottle?
Because his wife's dead.

How do you get a granny to shout "C––t!"?
Get another to shout "Bingo!"

ZOO POLITICS

"Hitler was a bad man. Winston Churchill was a good man. But if you were in a hot-air balloon with Hitler and Churchill, and you were losing altitude…"
Harry Hill

***Jade Goody** and **George Bush** are sitting in a pub with George's dog having a drink.*
A man walks in lifts up the dogs tail, shrugs and then walks out again.
Then another man does the same and then another.
When a fourth man does it, George stops him and says "You're the fourth person to do this. Why do people keep lifting his tail and having a look?"
To which the man replies, "There is a man outside telling people that there is a dog in here with two arseholes."

"You can't bomb the Afghans back to the Stone Age. They'll go, "Hey – upgrade!"
Robin Williams

"As you know, Saddam Hussein was hung. Or that's what he'd like to tell the ladies."
Jay Leno

D'OHVAL OFFICE

Top 10 reasons why I, Homer Simpson, should be the next President:

10. *I'm smarter than the last guy.*
9. *With an oval office, I can't bump into anything.*
8. *Fox News is already on my side.*
7. *I will take full advantage of the free food that comes with the job.*
6. *I have enormous experience apologizing for failed decisions.*
5. *I will appoint a Secretary of Donuts.*
4. *I will be the Secretary of Donuts.*
3. *My middle name isn't Hussein ... anymore.*
2. *My vice president will be Mayor McCheese.*
1. *Kick-ass inauguration party! Bring a six pack and you're in.*

Late Night With David Letterman

"President Bush met with the Pope on Saturday. There was one awkward moment... when he asked the Pope, 'Hey, how's Mrs. Pope?'"

Jay Leno

"Man, I'd kill for a Nobel Peace Prize."
Steven Wright

"You wanna know something? I actually like George W Bush. In some ways, I'm the George W Bush of hip hop – nobody likes me, but I'm still gonna run it for the next four years."
50 Cent

"President Bush is in Europe preparing for the G8 Summit and he's very excited. He thinks it's a conference on vegetable juice."
David Letterman, The Late Show

"The right to bear arms is slightly less ludicrous than the right to arm bears."
Chris Addison, stand-up

"Pol Pot rounded up everyone who was intellectual and had them killed. And he could tell if they were intellectual by whether they wore glasses. If they're that clever, take them off when you see him coming."
Ricky Gervais

"George W Bush? Some men are born great. Some achieve greatness. And some get it as a graduation gift."
Robin Williams

"Hillary Clinton has chosen the Celine Dion song 'You & I' as her campaign theme. I understand Bill was leaning towards 'My Humps.'"
Jay Leno, US talkshow host

"Bill Clinton earned more than $10 million last year from giving speeches but says he gave half of it to charity. He gives the other half to her sister, Tiffany."
Conan O'Brien, US talkshow host

"At the final cabinet meeting Jack Straw told Tony Blair that he'd always be remembered for Northern Ireland, the 2012 Olympics and civil partnership. So presumably if you're a gay sprinter from Belfast he's the best Prime Minister ever."
Trever McDonald, News Knight

"IT'S OUR PRESIDENT'S BIRTHDAY. HE'S 61 TODAY. ALSO, SYLVESTER STALLONE IS 61 TODAY. BUT STALLONE AND BUSH DON'T HAVE MUCH IN COMMON. ONE'S A BAD ACTOR WHO MUMBLES AND BLOWS STUFF UP, AND THE OTHER IS SYLVESTER STALLONE."
Craig Ferguson

"Earlier this week, police defused a potentially massive car bomb parked in front of London's famed Piccadilly Circus. President Bush got a little confused. He called the new Prime Minister and made sure all the animals and clowns were safe."
Jay Leno, US talkshow host

"Arctic Monkeys really wake you up in the morning."

Gordon Brown tries to prove he's "down with the kids"

"Politicians know young people listen to us more than them. That's why David Cameron said he fancied me. He was just trying to be cool, but should stop it and get on with running the country."
Girls Aloud's Cheryl Cole on the Tory leader "getting down with the kids"

"I HAVE TOO MANY BEDROOMS AND FEEL BAD ABOUT IT. BUT NOT SO BAD THAT I'M PREPARED TO LET HOMELESS PEOPLE COME AND LIVE WITH ME."
Steve Coogan asked how green his house is

"Ann Widdecombe says she's a virgin for religious reasons. The reason being that god made her incredibly ugly."
Frankie Boyle

"I couldn't run for office. I've slept with far too many people."
George Clooney dismisses dabbling in politics

"Ex-President Jimmy Carter said George W Bush is the worst President in history. But Bush hit back with, 'No, that's not true. I was the worst in Math and English as well.'"
Jay Leno, US talkshow host

"I stand by this man because he stands for things. Not only for things, he stands on things. Things like aircraft carriers, and rubble, and recently flooded city squares. And that sends a strong message that no matter what happens to America she will always rebound with the most powerfully staged photo-ops in the world."
Comedian Stephen Colbert, roasting Bush

"Cats can get passports now. How do you think that makes Mohammed Al-Fayed feel?"
Jeff Green

ZOO PUB JOKES

Be king of the bar with our generous round of booze-related gags. Ideal accompaniment: booze.

JUST PLAIN NUTS

A man walks into a pub and goes up to the bar. As he orders his drink, a voice from the bowl of peanuts on the bar goes, "Like your shirt mate." Before he can react, he hears from the direction of the cigarette machine, "Never mind your shirt, you're an ugly bastard." "What the hell's going on?" he asks the barman. "Ah, well the peanuts are complementary but the cigarette machine's out of order."

GRUB AND A RUB

Bloke's walking past a pub and sees a sign: "Pies 50p, handjobs £1."
He goes in and sees the most gorgeous barmaid. He says, "Are you the one who gives handjobs for a quid?"
"Yep," she says.
"Well wash your hands then I want a pie."

"Someone asked me if I always drink whisky neat, I said, 'No – sometimes my shirt's hanging out.'"
Tommy Cooper

MAKE MINE A DOUBLE

A woman walks into a bar and asks for a double entendre. So the barman gives her one.

BRAND NAME BOOZE

A white horse walks into a bar.
Barman says "We've got a whisky named after you."
Horse goes, "What, Dave?"

ASKING FOR TROUBLE

A bra and a set of jump leads walk into a pub. The barman says to the bra, "I'm not serving you lot. You're off your tits and your mates look like they want to start something."

BEER GOGGLES

A married couple are discussing the best way to tighten their belts.
Margaret says: "For a start, you spend £20 a week on beer, so that'll stop."
John: "Wait a minute, you spend £30 on make-up and beauty products."
Margaret: "Yes, dear, but that's to make me look attractive."
John: "And what do you think the beer's for?"

"There's these machines now that tell you when to stop drinking... Cashpoint machines."

Harry Hill

William Shakespeare goes into a pub. The landlord says "Get out, you're bard."

TAKING THE PISS

Why are women like pub loos?
They're either vacant, engaged or full of crap.

NO SHIT

A hat and a turd go up to the bar but the barman won't serve them. "No way - you're off your head and he's steaming."

BEAR IT IN MIND

Polar bear walks into a pub. Goes up to the bar and says, "Pint of Guinness please... ... ... and some dry roasted peanuts." Barman replies, "Why the big pause?"
"Because I'm a polar bear."

NOBODY TO GO WITH

A skeleton walks into a pub. "Pint of lager, please barman. Oh, and a mop."

A WHISKY STRATEGY

A man runs into a pub and orders the three most expensive malt whiskys they have. The barman lines them up, but before he's finished pouring the third, the bloke downs the first in one. As he necks the second, the barman says to him, "You're in a hurry." The bloke replies, "You would be too if you had what I have." The barman says, "Oh, sorry to hear that mate, what have you got?" The bloke downs the final whisky and replies, "50p."

MIX AND MATCH

"I like my whisky like I like my women. A 16-year-old mixed up with coke."
Bobby Davro

An Englishman, Scotsman and Irishman walk into a pub. The barman says, "What is this, some kind of joke?"

TOO PC BY HALF

"Three blind mice walk into a pub. But they are all unaware of their surroundings, so to derive humour from it would be exploitative."
Bill Bailey

REVENGE IS BEST SERVED CHEAP

Bloke goes into the pub and asks for a pint.
The barman says, "Sure, that'll be a penny."
Bloke goes, "A penny? This is the cheapest pub in the world! OK, I'll have steak and chips as well."
Barman says, "Very good, sir. That'll be two pence."
Bloke goes, "You're joking! Where's the landlord?"
Barman says, "Upstairs, with my wife."
Bloke says, "What's he doing up there?"
Barman says, "Same as I'm doing to his business."

"My local's rough as anything. I went to the pub quiz the other night.
First question was 'What the fuck are you looking at?'"
Jack Dee

"A hotel mini-bar allows you to see into the future... and what a can of Pepsi will cost in 2020."
Rich Hall

QUACKERS

A bloke comes home from the pub one night with a duck under his arm.
He says, "This is the pig I've been shagging."
His wife says, "That's a duck."
The bloke says, "I was talking to the duck."

ZOO ANIMALS

Animals – pet them, love them, then laugh at them and eat them.

"Bullfighters should be made to go in drunk, without a sword and just wearing one of those Viking helmets that people wear. That's a fair fight."

Ricky Gervais on making bloodsports less cruel – to the animals, anyway

Where would you find an elephant with no legs?
Where you left it.

An old lady kept two pet monkeys for years. Eventually one of them died, then two days later the other passed away from grief. Because they'd been such great companions the old lady took them to be stuffed.
The taxidermist asked, "Would you like them mounted?"
"No, no. Holding hands will be fine."

What's got two legs and bleeds?
Half a dog

"If a dog's tail is still wagging, then how can that be rape?" **Marek Larwood**

EMPEROR PENGUIN STRIKES BACK

A penguin takes his car to a mechanic because there's a funny noise coming from under the bonnet.
"Leave it with me," says the mechanic. "Come back in 20 minutes."
So off goes the penguin. It's a pretty hot day, so on spotting an ice cream van, he goes and buys himself a 99. Now, penguins aren't very good at eating ice creams – the lack of opposable thumbs makes it tricky. So by the time the penguin has finished his 99, he is completely covered in ice cream. It is all over his beak and all over his flippers. Feeling a little sticky, he goes back to the garage.
"Oh, hello," says the mechanic, wiping his hands on a cloth.
"Hello," replies the penguin. "Was it anything serious?"
"Not really, but it looks like you've blown a seal."
"Oh no!" says the penguin, wiping his beak. "It's just ice cream."

I saw this bloke chatting up a cheetah, I thought. "he's trying to pull a fast one". Peter Kay

MUTT MINEFIELD

A war veteran's walking along the street, dragging his left foot behind him, when he encounters a man coming the other way, doing the same.
The first guy nods knowingly, points to his gammy leg and says,
"Falklands, 25 years ago."
The other guy replies, "Dog shit, 30 yards back there."

What do you do if an elephant comes through your window?
Swim!

THE LONG LEASH OF THE LAW

"If you're being chased by a police dog, try not to go through a tunnel, then on to a little seesaw, then jump through a hoop of fire. They're trained for that."
Milton Jones

ANIMAL CRUELTY

A waiter asks a man, "May I take your order, sir?"
"Yes," the man replies. "I'm just wondering, exactly how do you prepare your chickens?"
"Nothing special, sir. We just tell them straight out that they're going to die."

What's the difference between a dog and a fox?
About five pints.

"Animal testing is a terrible idea. They get all nervous and give the wrong answers."

Stephen Fry

GET LEGLESS

Always keen on owning an unusual pet, a man buys what's advertised as a talking centipede from his local pet shop. After paying £5,000, he takes it home in its little box and puts it on top of the mantlepiece. Later that night he taps the box, slides it open and says: "Fancy coming down the pub for a pint?" The centipede doesn't answer. Raising his voice a little, he repeats the question. Still no answer. Convinced he's been conned out of £5,000, he angrily shouts: "Fancy coming down the pub for a pint?" The centipede sticks its head out and says: "I heard you the first time. I was putting my f-----g shoes on."

What do you call a bin bag full of mutilated laboratory monkeys?
Rhesus Pieces.
Comedy Central, *US TV show*

IT'S NO YOKE

The chicken and the egg are laying in bed.
The chicken's smoking a cigarette with a big satisfied smile on its face, while the egg is frowning and looking slightly annoyed.
The egg mutters, "Well, I guess that answers that riddle".

What's black and white and red all over?
Panda rape.

"I've got to go to the doctors to get a mole removed from my cock. Last time I fuck one of them things."
Mike Reid

What's got two grey legs and two brown legs?
An elephant with diarrhoea.

What's got four legs and goes "Boo"?
A cow with a cold.

What's the only animal with an arsehole in the middle of its back?
A police horse.

What's a shih-tzu?
One with no animals.

What do you do if a kitten spits at you?
Turn the grill down.

ANIMAL MAGIC

There was a magician on a cruise ship and he was really good. He was performing the highlight of his show when a parrot walked onstage and squawked, "It's in his sleeve!" The audience booed and the annoyed magician chased the bird away.

Next night, the magician was performing his highlight again, but in front of a smaller audience. The parrot walked onstage and declared, "It's in his pocket!" The audience booed again and the furious magician chased the bird away.

The next night, he was again performing his climactic trick, but to a tiny audience. On the lookout this time, the magician saw the parrot in the crowd. But before the parrot could ruin the trick, the boat crashed into a rock and sank.

The magician was lucky enough to find a board to hang on to. On the other end of the board was the parrot. They stared at each other for three full days, neither of them saying anything, when suddenly the parrot said, "I give up. What'd you do with the ship?"

FLIPPING OFF THE COPS

The police stop a car because the driver has 20 penguins in the back.

"You can't be driving around with a carload of penguins," says the copper, "Take them to the zoo."

The driver agrees.

The following day, the copper spots the same car – and again he has 20 penguins in the back.

"I thought I told you to take those to the zoo," says the policeman.

"I did," said the driver, "and today I'm taking them to the cinema."

"So I said 'Do you fancy a game of darts?'

He said 'OK then.'

I said 'Nearest to bull starts'.

He said 'Baa.'

I said 'Moo.'

He said 'You're closest'.

Peter Kay

"People say dogs aren't clever. But when did you see one tread in human shit?"
Billy Connolly

CANINE CAREER ADVICE

A dog goes into a hardware store and says, "I'd like a job, please."
The shop owner says, "We don't hire dogs. Why don't you join the circus?"
The dog says, "What would the circus want with a plumber?"

popbitch

"Don't you know lighting a cigarette the wrong way and inhaling stops the blood flowing to your private parts? And doing it more than once means you may never have an orgasm again."
Paris Hilton's latest flash of genius

"Say Laura, do you think I ought to sing something?"

GEORGE W BUSH TO HIS WIFE, AT A BONO-LED CHARITY CONCERT

"Years ago I saw an attractive girl at a bus stop who looked like an effeminate boy I went to school with. I thought he must've had a sex change, so I said "Hello Graham." It wasn't Graham. The poor girl was mortified."

Richard Madely on his most embarrassing moment

"The phone was ringing. I picked it up, and said 'Who's speaking please?' And a voice said, 'You are.'"
Tim Vine

"I tried to rob a department store... with a pricing gun. I said, 'Give me all the money, or I'm marking down everything in the store.'"
Steven Wright

"The next thing I knew, someone was waking me up saying, 'Mr Vegas, maybe you should get dressed.' I was in the hotel reception, naked from the waist down."

JOHNNY VEGAS ON HIS LATEST GUINNESS-FUELLED SCRAPE

"ONE IN FIVE PEOPLE IN THE WORLD IS CHINESE. AND THERE ARE FIVE PEOPLE IN MY FAMILY, SO IT MUST BE ONE OF THEM. IT'S EITHER MY MUM OR MY DAD. OR MY OLDER BROTHER COLIN. OR MY YOUNGER BROTHER HO CHAN CHU. BUT I THINK IT'S COLIN."
Tim Vine

"I go to lots of overseas places, like Canada."
Britney Spears. NB: she's American

"My dad used to say, 'Always fight fire with fire.' Which is probably why he was thrown out of the fire brigade."
Harry Hill

"I went up to the airport information desk. I said, 'How many airports are there in the world?'"
JIMMY CARR

"I saw this sign on the Underground next to the escalator saying: Dogs Must Be Carried. Could I find a dog anywhere? Could I fuck."
Dave Spikey

"DISNEYWORLD IN FLORIDA IS MY FAVOURITE PLACE. I FUCKING LOVE MICKEY MOUSE AND EVERY TIME I SEE THE CINDERELLA CASTLE, IT'S MY DREAM. I'D LOVE TO LIVE THERE."

PAUL GASCOIGNE: REALIST

"I walked into HMV the other day, and asked the assistant, 'Do you have anything by The Doors?' 'Yes,' he said. 'Two buckets and a fire extinguisher.'"
Tim Vine

"Most dentists' chairs go up and down. The one I was in went backwards and forwards. I thought, 'This is unusual.' And the dentist said to me, 'Mr Vine, get out of the filing cabinet.'"

Tim Vine

"Politician, woman, lobster, grass... That's it. No, wait! The sex of a fish. The big sex of a sports fish. Or maybe the little sex of a sports fish. A stickleback. You know what I'm saying?"

Eric Cantona, asked to describe himself in five words

"I went to the dentist. He said, 'Say aaah.' I said, 'Why?' He said, 'My dog's died.'"
Tim Vine

"My most embarrassing moment was once when I showed a holiday video to my entire family and forgot there was a point where I flashed. I only realised a second before it happened and couldn't get to the remote in time. My sister screamed and my mum said 'Ooh, that's changed.'"

Simon Pegg relives a post-holiday trauma

"I stopped a man from Wigan in the street on the way to the football and I asked him, 'How do you get to the JJB stadium?' And he said, 'Me brother takes me.'"

Dave Spikey

"I love the way the Brits treat me – not like an airhead but as the businesswoman I am."

"BUSINESSWOMAN" PARIS HILTON THREATENS TO MOVE TO BRITAIN.

"I KNEW I WAS GOING BALD WHEN IT WAS TAKING LONGER AND LONGER TO WASH MY FACE."

Harry Hill

David Beckham is celebrating. "Forty-three days, 43 days!" he shouts happily. Posh asks him why he's celebrating.
He answers " I've done this jigsaw in only 43 days."
"And that's good?" asks Posh.
"You bet," says David. "It says three to six years on the box."

"He looks like a fish up a tree. Out of his depth."

PAUL MERSON'S LATEST PUNDITRY GEM

**"A DIY enthusiast walks into his local library and asks: 'Do you have any books on shelves?'
The girl behind the counter said: 'They're all on shelves'."**

TAM COWAN, *DAILY RECORD*

"No-one deserves to be booed. Well some people do. Like Myra Hindley or Anne Robinson."

Big Brother's Glyn equates serial child killer to ginger gameshow hostess

"I was doing a gig the other day and got talking to a girl in the front row. I asked her name and she said, 'it's Pataka'. I said 'that's a name you don't hear every day'. To which she replied, 'actually I do'."

JIMMY CARR

"A cop pulled me over for running a stop sign. He said, 'Didn't you see the stop sign?' I said, 'Yeah, but I don't believe everything I read'."

STEVEN WRIGHT

"My son Foster is a fan of the sport. He was a goaltender. His elder brother was a defenseman."

Liverpool's American owner George Gillett impresses Anfield with his soccerball knowledge

"Yeah, I had to do a karaoke song. No-one escapes that little initiation rite. I did 'I'll Stand By You'. I don't even know who sings it, I just went for an easy one."

NOTE TO ASHLEY COLE: YOUR WIFE'S BAND GIRLS ALOUD HAD A NO 1 WITH THAT TUNE

"I'm so hot at the moment, I can turn anything on – animal, plant or mineral."

Modest mineral-brained Paris Hilton

"*Deal Or No Deal* might as well be called *Who Wants To Be A Millionaire For Thick People*. **'Do you know anything?' 'No'. 'Can you open a box?' 'Yes'. 'Alright then'. Then Noel Edmonds starts pacing the floor like a creepy lizard wearing spray-on trousers. And he keeps saying things like, 'Oh, you're playing a very shrewd game here.' Shrewd? I'm pointing at a box!"**

Russell Howard, Mock The Week

"THE THING I'VE NOTICED ABOUT THIS WORLD CUP IS THAT IT HAS A VERY INTERNATIONAL FEEL TO IT."

PERCEPTIVE PUNDITRY FROM FIVE'S JIMMY ARMFIELD

"So I went down the local supermarket, I said 'I want to make a complaint, this vinegar's got lumps in it', he said 'Those are pickled onions'."

PETER KAY

The fairer sex. Also the funnier one.

What's the difference between a woman on her period and a terrorist?

YOU CAN NEGOTIATE WITH A TERRORIST

"I've got no problem buying tampons. I'm a modern man. But apparently, they're not a 'proper present'."

Jimmy Carr

What do you call a room full of women, half with PMS, half with yeast infections?

A WHINE AND CHEESE PARTY

"I met a Dutch girl with inflatable shoes last week, phoned her up to arrange a date but unfortunately she'd popped her clogs".

Peter Kay

How do you make five pounds of fat look good?

Give it a nipple

A man approached a very beautiful woman in a large supermarket and asked, "You know, I've lost my wife here in the supermarket. Can you talk to me for a couple of minutes?"
"Why?"
"Because every time I talk to a beautiful woman my wife appears out of nowhere."

Q: What is the similarity between PlayStations and breasts?
A: Both are made for children, but used by adults.

What's the difference between BSE and PMT?
One is mad cow disease while the other has something to do with beef.

A blonde with two burnt ears goes to the doctor, who asks what has happened.
"The phone rang, and I accidentally picked up the iron."
"What about the other one?"
"They called back."

A guy is walking past a bus stop and says to a woman "Can I smell your ct?"**
"Fuck off, no, you can't smell my ct!" the woman yells back at him,**
"Oh," he replies, looking confused, "must be your feet then".

A man is speeding down a narrow mountain road, when a woman comes hurtling round the corner. He swerves to avoid her, but as she passes she leans out the window and screams "PIG!"
Astonished, the man turns and yells back, "BITCH!" as he reaches the bend and crashes into a pig.

Why are hurricanes named after women? Because when they come, they're wild and wet, and when they go they take your house and car with them.

Why do men die before their wives?
They want to.

How can you tell if your wife is dead? The sex is the same but the dishes pile up.

What do a woman and Kentucky Fried Chicken have in common? By the time you've finished on the breast and thighs, all you have left is a greasy box for the bone.

**The last fight we had was my fault. My wife asked, "What's on the TV?"
I said, "Dust."**

Three women went out drinking, and decided to have a contest of who could get the drunkest. The next day the women all got together. The first woman said, "I drove my car into a ditch."
The second woman said, "I blew chunks."
The third woman said, "I burned down my house."
After they all had told their stories, the third woman said, "I guess I won."
The second woman replied, "You don't understand, Chunks is my dog."

Q: Why are bachelors thin, and married men fat?
A: Bachelors come home, check to see what's in the fridge, and go to bed. Married men come home, check to see what's in the bed, and go the fridge.

Did you know there are female hormones in beer? If you drink too much, it makes you talk shit and drive badly.

Doctors have found that single women can't fart. They don't have an arsehole until they get married.

How do you give a woman more freedom?
Make the kitchen larger.

"The other day I sent my girlfriend a huge pile of snow. I rang her up, I said 'Did you get my drift?'."

Peter Kay

If your dog's barking at the back door and your wife's knocking at the front door whom would you let in first?
The dog, because he'll shut up once he's in.

A taxi pulls up outside a lady's house. The cabbie turns around and says: "That'll be £12."
The woman in the back has no money, so instead she pulls up her skirt and spreads her legs. "Can I pay with this?" she asks.
"Christ!" the cabbie replies. "Haven't you got anything smaller?"

A beautiful, voluptuous woman goes to see a gynaecologist. Right away he tells her to undress. After she has disrobed he strokes her thigh.
As he does, he says to the woman: "Do you know what I'm doing?"
"Yes," she says, "you're checking for any abrasions or dermatological abnormalities."
"Correct," says the doctor.
He then fondles her breasts. "Do you know what I'm doing now", he says.
"Yes," says the woman, "you're checking for any lumps or breast cancer."
"That's right," replies the doctor. He then proceeds to have sex with
her. "Do you know," he pants, "what I'm doing now?"
"Yes," she says. "You're getting herpes."

What's the white stuff you find in the bottom of girls' undies?
Clitty litter.

What does a woman of 40 have between her breasts that a woman of 20 doesn't?
A belly-button.

I haven't spoken to my girlfriend for 18 months. I don't like to interrupt her.

A study in the UK showed that the kind of male face a woman finds attractive can differ on where a woman is in her menstrual cycle. For instance, if she is ovulating, she is attracted to men with rugged, masculine features. And if she's menstruating she's more prone to be attracted to a man with scissors shoved in his temple.

ZOO HOLLYWOOD

"I hope all my new work will help producers get past my hotness."

Jessica Alba: immodest but factually accurate

"I once tried to chat up Kate Winslet. She either didn't hear me or she ignored me."

Will Ferrell shrugs off a ginger blow-out

"I love to put on lotion. Sometimes I'll watch TV and go into a lotion trance for an hour, just rubbing it in."

ANGELINA JOLIE. WE'RE IN A TRANCE JUST THINKING ABOUT IT

"She gets her boobs out all the time and it's considered art."

Jordan gets jealous of Sienna Miller

"There's nothing worse than a sex scene where someone's got a T-shirt on or a strategic sheet over them. It's unrealistic. If you're going to do it, do it."

SIENNA MILLER VOWS TO GIVE US SOMETHING TO LOOK AT

"I'll pick out two outfits, one which is disgusting and one nice and I'll ask my 'friend' what they think. If they go for the revolting one, I cut them out of my life."

PARIS HILTON ON HOW SHE WEEDS OUT HER FRIENDS

"If I were a guy, I'd ask Cameron to marry me. She has the cutest, tightest butt and she's also a world-class belcher."

EVA MENDES ON CAMERON DIAZ, AND WHO ARE WE TO ARGUE?

"I read the book, read the script, saw the film and still don't understand it."

Sean Connery on why he turned down the role of Gandalf in *Lord Of The Rings*

"She has the naughtiest eyes in showbusiness. When she looks you straight in the eye, it's stunning."

Daniel Craig has a crush on his Bond boss Dame Judie Dench

"I got gashed above my right eye but just rubbed a little dirt on it and kept going. Chicks dig scars."

BRUCE WILLIS AFTER GETTING KICKED

"Fk this. I'll buy the f**king hotel."**

HOLLYWOOD BIG NOB HARVEY WEINSTEIN, AFTER BEING TOLD THAT A CARIBBEAN PRIVATE BEACH WAS FOR HOTEL RESIDENTS ONLY

"I'm afraid sir, the fking hotel isn't for sale. Good day."**

HOTEL MANAGER'S ICE COOL REPLY

A good looking man walked into an agent's office in Hollywood and said "I want to be a movie star." Tall, handsome and with experience on Broadway, he had the right credentials.
The agent asked, "What's your name?"
The guy said, "My name is Penis van Lesbian."
The agent said, "Sir, I hate to tell you, but in order to get into Hollywood, you are going to have to change your name."
"I will NOT change my name! The van Lesbian name is centuries old, I will not disrespect my grandfather by changing my name. Not ever."
The agent said, "Sir, I have worked in Hollywood for years... you will NEVER go far in Hollywood with a name like Penis van Lesbian! I'm telling you, you will HAVE TO change your name or I will not be able to represent you."
"So be it! I guess we will not do business together" the guy said and he left the agent's office.
Five years later the agent opens an envelope sent to his office. Inside the envelope is a letter and a check for $50,000. The agent is awe-struck, who would possibly send him $50,000? He reads the letter enclosed...
'Dear Sir, Five years ago, I came into your office wanting to become an actor in Hollywood , you told me I needed to change my name. Determined to make it with my God-given birth name, I refused. You told me I would never make it in Hollywood with a name like Penis van Lesbian. After I left your office, I thought about what you said. I decided you were right. I had to change my name. I had too much pride to return to your office, so I signed with another agent. I would never have made it without changing my name, so the enclosed check is a token of my appreciation.

Thank you for your advice.
Sincerely,

Dick van Dyke

"People love me in my underwear. It's a public service. If I'm not in my underwear by page 50 of the script, I'm not happy."

WILL FERRELL EMBRACES SEMI-NUDE SCENES

"Sex scenes are easy. I don't have a problem with them. Actually it was quite liberating to be out in the desert, completely topless, with a beautiful Venezuelan guy."

Kiera Knightley recalls rude scenes in Domino. *Men worldwide curse the "beautiful Venezuelan" bit*

"I LOVE FILMING SEX SCENES WITH WOMEN."

Angelina Jolie's claim is music to our ears

ZOO READERS

Why do elephants drink? To forget.

SENT IN BY READER ALAN BUCK, CLEETHORPES

Two antennas met on a roof, fell in love and got married. The ceremony wasn't much, but the reception was excellent.

SENT IN BY READER DARREN HOLMES, PETERBOROUGH

Two peanuts walk into a bar and one was a salted.

SENT IN BY READER JEREMY M, GENEVA

Before bed one night, Arsene Wenger is trying to think of ways to get Arsenal's season back on track. As a last effort, he prays to God for guidance. God hears the Frenchman's whining and decides to take pity. Later that night Wenger suddenly awakes to see The Lord standing at the bottom of his bed. "Come forth my son!" says God. To which Wenger replies, "Fourth? We'll be lucky if we finish bloody sixth!"

SENT IN BY READER COLIN, PRESTON

Q: How does Michael Jackson pick his nose?
A: From a catalogue.

SENT IN BY READER ANDREW MEEK, BATH

Why have you never met a Jewish or Muslim morris dancer?
Because it takes a complete prick to be a Morris dancer.

FROM CUBAN DAVE, MANCHESTER

A Polish immigrant in Britain decides to go for an eye test.
After working his way down to the bottom line on the chart – CZWIXNOSTACZ – the optician says: "Well, can you read that?"
"Read it?" replies the Pole. "I went to school with his brother."

SENT IN BY READER DEACO, EDINBURGH

What do you call a bloke with three eyes? Seymour.

What do you call a Spaniard who's had his motor nicked? Carlos.

What do Viagra and Alton Towers have in common? They both make you stand around for an hour waiting for a two minute ride.

A Glastonbury Portaloo goes up to the bar and orders a pint of cider.
Barman says, "No way, you're steaming."

SENT IN BY ALEX, DERBY

A man says to his wife, "Put your coat on – I'm going to the pub." His wife says, "Ooh, lovely – are you taking me for a drink?" The man says, "No, I'm turning the heating off."

SENT IN BY READER JOHN BAIRD, SUNDERLAND

A doctor sits one of his female patients down and with a stern look on his face says, "I'm sorry to say the tests you had don't look good. It seems that you're suffering from cancer and Alzheimer's disease."
To which the lady replies, "Well, at least I don't have cancer!"

SENT IN BY READER JIMMY FALLEN, EDINBURGH

A feminist visited Kuwait several years before the Gulf War and noted that women customarily walked about 10 feet behind their husbands.
She returned to Kuwait recently and was surpised to see that the men now walked several yards behind their wives.
Approaching one of the women for an explanation, she said: "This is marvellous. What enabled women here to achieve this reversal of gender roles?"
"Land mines," came the reply.

SENT IN BY MR FINGER, BY EMAIL

A bloke says to his wife "Why don't you tell me when you orgasm?" She replies, "I don't like ringing you at work."

SENT IN BY ALAN LANSDOWNE, RENFREW

A driver stopped for speeding. When asked for his occupation he replies, "Rectum stretcher". "What on earth is that?" asks the cop. Driver says "You put one finger in, then two, then a hand etc until it's 6ft wide." Cop asks, "What do you do with a 6ft arsehole?" Driver replies, "Give it a uniform and a fucking speed gun."

SENT IN BY ALAN LANSDOWNE, RENFREW

What's worse than having termites in your piano? Crabs on your organ.

SENT IN BY NICK F, CHELMSFORD

Why do Buddhists refuse novocaine during root canal work? Because they want to transcend dental medication.

SENT IN BY READER JAMIE LYNCH, BURY

One night, a man rolls over in bed and gives his wife a big, knowing grin. Immediately realising his intentions she says, "Not tonight darling. I have an appointment with the gynaecologist tomorrow morning and I want to stay fresh and clean."
Disappointed, the husband rolls over and tries to get to sleep. A few minutes later, he rolls over and prods his wife again. "Tell me, do you have a dentist appointment tomorrow, too?"

SENT IN B.Y DAZZLA B, BY EMAIL

Why do brides dress in white?
So they match the rest of the appliances.

SENT IN BY PAUL T, LINCS

Two blokes are in a barber's shop. They've both just finished having a shave, and the barber reaches for some aftershave. The first bloke yells, "Hey! Don't put that cheap crap on me! My wife will think I've been in a brothel!" The second bloke turns to the barber and says, "Put it on me. My wife doesn't know what the inside of a brothel smells like."

SENT IN BY READER RYAN WILLARD, HORSHAM

MEAT HABIT

What's black and white, then black and brown, then black and black?
A nun roasting on a spit.

SENT IN BY SHANKSY, WEST YORKS

After all the revelations about him in the press, David Hasselhoff has said he only wants to be know as The Hoff. I guess he just doesn't want the hassel any more.

SENT IN BY READER DAVE, CONGLETON

A man goes to confession and says, "Father, I have been with a loose woman." The priest says, "Who was the woman?" The man says, "I can't tell, Father. I don't want to ruin her reputation." The priest says, "I'm sure to find out, so you may as well say. Was it Brenda O'Malley?" The man won't tell. "Was it Patricia Kelly?" The man won't tell. "Was it Liz Shannon?" The man won't tell. "Was it Cathy Morgan?" The man won't tell. "Was it Fiona McDonald?" The man won't tell. The priest sighs and says, "You're steadfast, and I admire that. But you've sinned and must atone. You cannot attend church for three months. Be off with you." The man walks back to his pew. His mate slides over and whispers, "What did you get?" The man says, "Three months' vacation and five good leads."

SENT IN BY MRS WINTY, HARPENDEN

What's white and can't climb trees? A fridge.

SENT IN BY READER TOM PRINCE, BIRMINGHAM

RING OF TRUTH

A man goes to his GP and says, "Doc please help me! I've got a problem." The doctor examines him and finds the man has a red ring around his penis. He gives him an ointment to rub on the problem area and tells him to come back the next day.
"It's all cleared up!" the man reports when he returns. "But what was that medication you gave me?"
"Lipstick remover."

SENT IN BY BIG SI, ABERSOCH

Two blokes are talking. First bloke says, "I tried to kill myself yesterday by taking 1,000 aspirins." Second bloke says, "What happened?" First bloke says, "Well, after the first two I felt better."

SENT IN BY READER FRASER CLARK, GLENROTHES

A student visits a Bangkok massage parlour. A sexy masseuse asks him to strip to his boxers and lie down. She starts to massage the young man's chest – then looks down and notices his bulge. She says, "Ah, you want wank?" He says, "Yes please!" She says, "OK, you stay here" – then leaves the room. The student thinks, "This is what gap year holidays are all about – getting tugged off by a fit Thai bird!" Two minutes pass and he begins to get anxious about where she's got to. Another minute later the masseuse sticks her head round the door. She says, "You finish yet?"

SENT IN BY READER COLIN VEITCH

A British couple are on holiday in Jerusalem when the man's ever-nagging wife suddenly drops dead. The undertaker says, "It'll cost £10,000 to have the body flown back to Britain, or we can bury her here in The Holy Land for £250." The man says, "I'd like the body flown home." The undertaker says, "Why spend all that money when we can offer a special burial here for a fraction of the price?" The man says, "A bloke died here many years ago. This is where he was buried. Three days later, he rose from the dead. I'm not taking any chances."

SENT IN BY READER DAVID GILCHRIST, BELLSHILL

Viagra is now available in powder form to put in your tea. It won't enhance your sexual performance, but it does stop your biscuits going soft.

SENT IN BY READER BELLY, ORMSKIRK

A Catholic, a Baptist and a Mormon are bragging about the size of their families. The Catholic says, "I have four boys and my wife is pregnant. One more son and I'll have a basketball team." The Baptist says, "I can beat that. I have 10 boys, and my wife is pregnant. One more son and I'll have a football team." The Mormon says, "That's nothing. I have 17 wives. One more and I'll have a golf course."

SENT IN BY READER MARK HEWITT, CONNAH'S QUAY

A man presented his girlfriend with three choices of condom – gold, silver, or bronze.
"Silver," she said.
"Why not gold?"
"Because I want you to come second for once."

SENT IN BY READER TOMMY F, NORTHAMPTON

I was just reading through that book 50 Things To Do Before You Die, *and I was really surprised that none of them was "Shout for help!"*

SENT IN BY READER CLIFF MACK

A man wakes up and says to his wife, "I had a wet dream about you last night!" "Aww, did you?" she says. "Yeah, I dreamt you were hit by a bus and I pissed myself laughing!"

SENT IN BY READER MATTHEW DREW, BRISTOL

A three-year-old was examining his testicles while taking a bath.
"Mom," he asked, "Are these my brains?"
Mother replied: "Not yet."

SENT IN BY READER BENNY B

What's the difference between Sir Alex Ferguson and James Brown?
Fergie will be playing Giggs this year.

SENT IN BY READER CLIFF TAYLOR, BRENTFORD

A little girl turns to her mum and says, "Mummy, Billy next door has a willy just like a peanut." Her mum says, "Do you mean it's really tiny?" The little girl says, "No, I mean it's really salty."

SENT IN BY READER STEVE LAKE, CLYDEBANK

What do you say to a girl with no arms or legs? Nice tits.

SENT IN BY READER ROB BAYLISS, MIDDLESEX

Q What did the elephant say to the naked man?
A How do you breathe through that thing?

SENT IN BY READER ALEX S, YEOVIL

A duck walks into a bar and asks: "Got any Bread?"
Barman: "No."
Duck: "Got any bread?"
Barman: "No."
Duck: "Got any bread?"
Barman: "No, we have no bread."
Duck: "Got any bread?"
Barman: "No, I just said. We haven't got any bread!"
Duck: "Got any bread?"
Barman: "What are you, deaf? We haven't got any fucking bread. Ask me
again and I'll nail your fucking beak to the bar!"
Duck: "Got any nails?"
Barman: "No"
Duck: "Got any bread?

SENT IN BY DREW JAMESON, GLASGOW

How many emo kids does it take to change a lightbulb? None, they'd rather sit in the dark and cry about how everyone hates them.

SENT IN BY READER JAKE BRANCH

Tiger Woods drives his new Merc into an Irish petrol station. An attendant says hello but, being a bit dim, doesn't recognise him. As Woods gets out of the car, two tees fall out of his pocket. The attendant says, "What are those?" Woods says, "Tees. They're for resting my balls on when I drive." The attendant says, "Jesus, those fellas at Mercedes think of everything."

SENT IN BY READER ALAIN

George W Bush is rehearsing a speech for the Olympics. He begins with,
"Ooo! Ooo! Ooo! Ooo! Ooo!" His assistant says, "Sir, those are the Olympic rings. Your speech is underneath."

SENT IN BY READER TOM MORRIS, ST IVES

A sad-looking bloke walks into a pub and sits at the bar, glumly sipping whisky. The barman asks him what's the matter.
"My life is awful," the man says. "Every night I play Trivial Pursuit with my wife, and every night she beats me."
"Well, why don't you just stop playing Trivial Pursuit?" the barman asks.
"I love the game," the man says. "I'm a genius. I never lose."
The barman's confused. "I thought you just said your wife beats you."
"Well," the man says, "she's a bad loser."

SENT IN BY READER PATRICK H

What does an Essex girl say after having sex?
"What team do you guys play for?"

SENT IN BY READER WINTY, HERTS

What's small, furry and hates sex?
The injured badger in the boot of my car.

SENT IN BY READER ALEX S, TAUNTON

I asked my wife what she wanted for her birthday and she replied: "Something to run around in." So I brought her a tracksuit.

SENT IN BY READER JIMMY G

A bloke's queuing in Tesco when he notices that the rather fit blonde behind him has just raised her hand and smiled hello to him. She looks familiar but he can't quite place where he knows her from.
So he says, "Sorry do you know me?"
She replies, "I may be mistaken, but I think you might be the father of one of my children."
His mind shoots back to the one and only time he's been unfaithful to his wife. "Christ!" he says "Don't tell me you're that stripper from my stag night? The one I shagged on the snooker table in front of my mates, whilst the other stripper whipped me and stuck a cucumber up my ass?"
"No," she replies, "I'm your son's English teacher."

SENT IN BY GARETH "G-MAN" JONES, BY EMAIL

What's the difference between a Ritz biscuit and a lesbian? One's a snack cracker, the other's a crack snacker.

SENT IN BY READER MARK HEWITT, CONNAH'S QUAY

Teacher notices little Billy is not paying attention during maths class. Trying to catch him out she shouts out to him, "Billy, what's 9 and 15 and 37?"
Quick as a flash Billy shouts back, "Sky One, Discovery and BBC News 24, Miss".

SENT IN BY READER SIM GRIFFITHS

A man suggests to his missus, "Darling, shall we try swapping positions tonight?"
"Great idea," she replies. "You stand by the ironing board while I sit on the sofa and fart."

SENT IN BY READER NOAH, SOLIHULL

A man walks into a bar and orders a triple scotch. As the barman pours it, he remarks, "That's quite a heavy drink. What's the problem?"
After quickly downing it, the man replies, "I found my wife in bed with my best friend."
"Wow," says the barman, giving him a refill on the house. "What did you do about it?"
"I walked over to my wife, looked her in the eye, told her to pack her stuff and get the hell out."
"That makes sense," nods the barman. "And what about your best friend?"
"I looked him right in the eye and yelled, 'Bad dog.'"

SENT IN BY READER DOM, ALTRINCHAM

A guy comes home early and finds his wife in bed with another man.
"What the hell are you doing?" shouts the irate husband.
"See?" the wife says to the man lying beside her. "I told you he doesn't know a thing about sex."

SENT IN BY READER MARK HEWITT, CONNAH'S QUAY

ZOO INTERNATIONAL

"Not really a loss not having the Swiss on your side in a war, is it? See the little knives they carry? 'Woah, back off, he's got some tweezers…'"

RICKY GERVAIS

"This is the first time in my lifetime that Irish people are able to go: 'What? You're going to England? It's full of terrorists. Come to Ireland. We've no terrorists at all. They're all playwrights now'."

Dara O'Brian, stand-up

"North Korea and Japan have never got on. I don't think they ever will. You know what the problem is? Neither side can say sorry."

JIMMY CARR

"Unlike Englishmen, I don't need to drink alcohol before I can dance. It's natural to me, it's what I do. I'm the best dancer and the best dresser at Man United."

Cristiano Ronaldo makes himself ever more lovable

"Americans are building a new tower on the site of the World Trade Centre and looking at ways of making it terrorist-proof. They should just build a giant mosque. They wouldn't fly into that. Or, even better, a runway."
Frankie Boyle

Italians. Slanty little Is. Oh no, that's italics.

MILTON JONES

"My top tip for World Cup commentary? Don't start speaking until at least five seconds after a national anthem. It might not be finished."

ITV'S CLIVE TYDLESLEY. HIS OTHER TIP? "DON'T MENTION THE WAR"

"It is cool. It means people think about me. Now I have the recognition I deserve."

Hakan Yakin's chuffed to be named "most arrogant player' in the Swiss league

"The most famous football player in the world, Michael Beckham."

Commentator on US TV channel ABC

"In my country you must be at least 18-year-old for watch scenes containing uncaged women and for view explicit sexytime you must be at least three."

Borat on film ratings in Kazakhstan

"I struggle to understand English women because they talk too fast, so I just give them my number and then they go away."

WIGAN'S SENEGALESE STRIKER HENRI CAMARA

"Everything in England is shut at 5pm, there is nothing to do, nowhere to go. I just got bored."

JOSE ANTONIO REYES REVEALS THE PROBLEMS OF LIFE IN ENGLAND

"There are two taps over here, one for hot and one for cold. At home we have one tap for both. Also, I don't know why you have carpet in the bathroom."

Polish import Grzegorz Rasiak on his troubles settling in Southampton

"All those who believe in psychokinesis, raise my hand."
Steven Wright

What do you say to a German fan with a good-looking woman on his arm? Nice tattoo.

"I STILL DON'T GET CRICKET. IT'S DIFFICULT TO UNDERSTAND A GAME THAT LASTS FIVE DAYS AND HAS A TEA-TIME."

Thierry Henry explains the limits to his Englishness

"I think Iran and Iraq simply had a war as their names are so similar they kept getting each other's post."
Paul Merton, Have I Got News For You

"They say travel broadens the mind, except with Americans, where it tends to widen the arse".

Jimmy Carr, stand-up

"Irish people love Muslims. They have taken a lot of heat off us. Before, we were 'the terrorists' but now, we're 'the Riverdance people'."

ANDREW MAXWELL

ZOO LAUGHTER LINES

"In this country we spend as much on food in one week as a family in the Third World does in a year. I just can't help but think we're being overcharged for our groceries."

JIMMY CARR

"God created the Universe and man on day one. And then, on the second day, he created light. So he did all that in the dark – how cool is that?"

RICKY GERVAIS

"I've got a friend who used to self-harm because he was bullied. I used to think 'Whose side are you on?'"

JIMMY CARR

"TV weather bugs me, like when they put cloud and lightning on the board. I know what clouds look like! Just tell me – I'll understand!"

BILLY CONNOLLY

"I don't do enough for charity. I do it a bit, but you can always do more. But I look at it like this – it's a pain, isn't it?"

RICKY GERVAIS

"Those people who get implants, it's so depressing. The root of that is they want more attention, but they always go for the most obvious place. If you really want more attention, why not get implants in your eyes, and then move your eyes down to where your nipples used to be, put your breasts upon your head. Everybody will pay attention."

* FROM THE DVD *DYLAN MORAN: LIVE*

"Cutting carrots with the Grim Reaper? That's just dicing with death."

TIM VINE

"What's the odd one out – 15, 20, 25, 27, 30, 35 or 40? You don't need to be Carol Vorderman to say the obvious answer is 27, but you'd be wrong – it's actually 30. All the others come with fried rice."

TAM COWAN, *DAILY RECORD*

"I said to the taxi driver, 'King Arthur's Close.' He said, 'Don't worry, we'll lose him at the next set of lights.'"

TOMMY COOPER

"Have you ever wondered why, when you're sick, there's always diced carrots in it? I've never eaten diced carrots in my life. I've come to the conclusion that it's not drink that makes you sick – it's diced bloody carrots."

BILLY CONNOLLY

"Genius is 10% inspiration, 90% respiration. You'd be surprised how many geniuses forget to breathe."

STEPHEN COLBERT, US COMEDIAN

"I always keep a lighter in my pocket. I don't smoke, I just like certain slow songs."

JIMMY CARR

"I LIVE QUITE NEAR A SPECIAL SCHOOL. THERE'S A SIGN ON THE ROAD OUTSIDE THAT SAYS 'SLOW CHILDREN' I THOUGHT, 'THAT CAN'T BE GOOD FOR THEIR SELF-ESTEEM.' BUT THEN AGAIN, NONE OF THEM CAN READ."

FROM THE DVD

JIMMY CARR LIVE

"I come from a very traditional family. When I was seven, my Uncle Terry hanged himself on Christmas Eve. My family didn't take his body down until the sixth of January."

NICK DOODY

"What they don't tell you about taking acid is that it's dull. But all these TV reviewers use it as a metaphor for shows that are wacky. "It's like Terry And June *on acid." Can you imagine that? It'll be Terry staring at the floral pattern on a plate for four days."*

BILL BAILEY

"I like magic mushrooms but I hate mushrooms. Why can't God make magic peas instead?"

STEVE HUGHES

"A woman with a clipboard came up to me in the street and asked if I could spare a few minutes for cancer research. I said, 'Fine, but we won't get much done.'"

JIMMY CARR

"In ice skating, why's it called a camel spin? I've never seen a camel go round and round on one leg on ice."

ALAN DAVIES

"Let's hear it for my wife's Aunt Rosie, who was 80 yesterday. I only realised she was that old when I told a knock-knock joke and she refused to answer until I'd shown three different types of ID. Last week, she said: 'The best present I could ask for is to be surrounded by my pals.' So we took her to the cemetery..."

TAM COWAN, DAILY RECORD

"Parents say stupid things, don't they? 'Can I go out on my bike?' 'What? Bike? I'll give you bike!' 'But I've already got a bike...'"

BILLY CONNOLLY

"I went to a restaurant yesterday, and ordered my meal in French. Surprised everyone – it was a Chinese restaurant."

TOMMY COOPER

"Know who I blame for the rise of drugs in schools? The supply teachers."

JIMMY CARR

"A policeman pulled me over and said, 'Would you please blow into this bag, sir?' I said, 'What for, Officer?' He says, 'My chips are too hot.'"

TOMMY COOPER

"There's so many cookery shows on telly that you can't get away from them. I got a thing to apply for my new TV license in the post, and I thought fuck it, I'll just buy a cookbook."

JACK DEE

"The airlines are saying no more hair gels, shampoos, make-up or hair spray allowed in carry-on bags. Who's attacking us? Drag queens?"

JAY LENO, US TALKSHOW HOST

"Police arrested two kids yesterday. One was drinking battery acid, the other was eating fireworks. They charged one and let the other one off."

TOMMY COOPER

"Friend of mine, Irish chap, opened a fish and chip shop. Customer walked in and asked for fish and chips twice. Fella said, 'I heard you the first time.'"

RONNIE CORBETT

"Wearing a Nazi costume wasn't the cleverest thing Prince Harry's ever done. Putting himself forward as a member of the Master Race with ginger hair and only one O-level."

GRAHAM NORTON

"I was a pathetic drunk. I'd get so drunk that when the cops pulled me over I'd start dancing to their lights, thinking I'd made it to another club."

BILL HICKS

"This waiter brought me my lobster last night. I said, 'Just a minute, it's only got one claw.' He said, 'It's been in a fight.' I said, 'Well, bring me the winner.'"

TOMMY COOPER

"I'll always remember the first girl I held. You never forget your first hostage."

JIMMY CARR

"All women have a skeleton in the closet. All women. Even the shy, quiet ones. Some of them got cemeteries. You open the door and ravens and shit fly out."

EDDIE MURPHY

ACCIDENTAL PORN

CROSS SAFELY

HARD SEAT

SCRATCHY BARK

HARD AS A ROCK

IMPRESSIVE ERECTION

REMARKABLE BUSH

WET DREAM

OVERGROWN POLE

DARK CREVICE

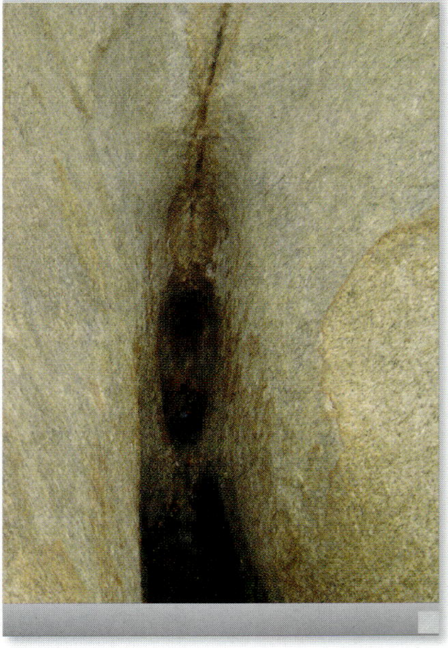

BEARING UP

A RUB AND A SQUIRT

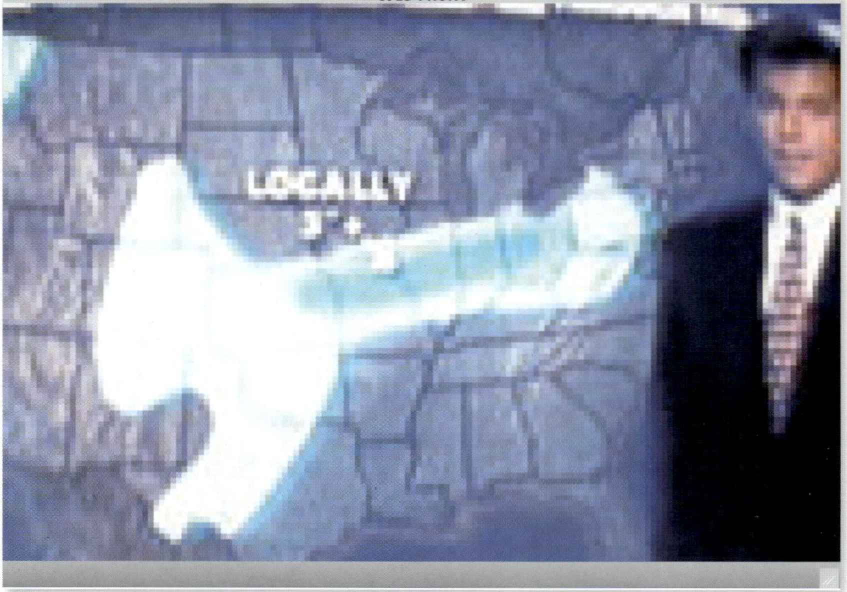

COLD FRONT

LEMON WITH A TWIST

NEEDLE PLANT

NOT A PEACH

PRICKLY PLANT

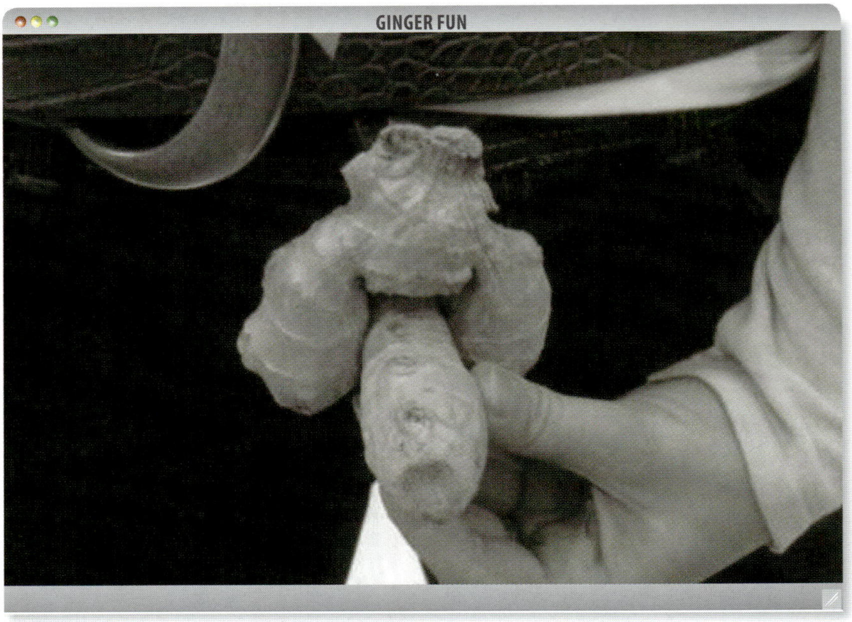
GINGER FUN

BIG BOY

"Andy Murray has agreed a £1million sponsorship with Highland Spring. But he's not the first tennis star to sign a deal with mineral water companies. I'm talking, of course, about Fred Perrier and Evian Lendl."

"And what about the Spanish woman giving birth to twins at age 67? Apparently she's ruled out breast-feeding. She's scared they'll get germs off the floor."

TAM COWAN, DAILY RECORD

[To bloke in the audience] *"Do you believe in God, sir? No? I don't blame you, you've been dealt a very poor hand."*

HARRY HILL

"I phoned a takeaway last week and asked, 'Do you deliver?' They said, 'No, we do chicken, beef and fish.'"

PETER KAY

"I'm on a whisky diet. Last week I lost three days."

TOMMY COOPER

"I bumped into a friend coming out of the doctor. 'You look sad,' I said. He said, 'I've been diagnosed as a kleptomaniac.' 'So what did the doctor say?' 'He's given me some tablets. If they don't work, can I get him a CD player.'

RONNIE CORBETT

"My father died while fucking. He came and went at the same time."

RICHARD PRYOR

"We got so much food in America, we're even allergic to it. How could someone be allergic to food? Do you think anybody in Rwanda's lactose intolerant?"

CHRIS ROCK

"I was on the cover of the Big Issue *so I had to buy it. The guy said, 'I love you in* Phoenix Nights.*' I said, 'How've you seen it? I'll have my pound back, you devious bastard.'"*

PETER KAY

"I'm not going into a whole thing about how I hate garages. I think a lot of things they do are wonderful. I think it's great the way they provide black buckets for your dead flowers."

* FROM THE DVD *JACK DEE: LIVE AND UNCUT*

"I sent my daughter to a private school. That's 73 grand's worth of education. And now she wants to be an actor? I've asked her to do porn and give me the money back."

JANEY GODLEY, SCOTTISH STAND-UP

"I like to melt together four Chunky Kit-Kats so when you eat them you can pretend you're a tiny pixie."

* FROM THE DVD *BILL BAILEY LIVE: PART TROLL*

"Dom Joly was at school with Bin Laden and still remembers those happy playground games like Tag, Stuck In The Mud and Die Infidel Die."

ANGUS DEAYTON, *WOULD I LIE TO YOU?*

"I've had a difficult couple of weeks. I grew a beard. It turned out to be ginger. Bit disappointing. Only acceptable form of racism on the planet and I grew it on my face."

ALISTAIR BARRIE, STAND-UP

"I feel sorry for whales – they live in the sea and breathe air. That's like us walking with a big tank of water on your head. And they keep trying to get ashore, but we keep pushing them back."

LEE EVANS

"Michael Jackson's claiming racism. Honey, you got to pick a race first."

ROBIN WILLIAMS

"Why did the Scots invent steam trains? So they could leave. They invented TV so they could look at other places."

AL MURRAY

"We don't need gun control, we need bullet control. If every bullet cost $5,000, people would think before they shot someone. 'Man, if I could afford to, I would blow your fucking head off. I'm a get me another job, I'm gonna work overtime and then you're a dead man. You better hope I can't get no bullets on credit.'"

CHRIS ROCK

"You meet a guy. He likes you and you like him. And it comes to the end of the night and you're not going to do anything. And he's like, 'OK.' After that he don't like you no more, but he still wants *to fuck you. So he waits and he waits. He waits three months and you finally do it and it's good and you go, 'I'm yours.' And he's like 'Fuck you, bitch. Fuck you and your pussy.'"*

EDDIE MURPHY FROM THE DVD *RAW*

"I woke up in the ambulance and there was nothing but white people staring at me. I was like, 'Ain't this a bitch, I died and ended up in the wrong heaven.'"

* FROM THE DVD *RICHARD PRYOR: LIVE IN CONCERT*

"I'm not homophobic. I'm not afraid of my house".

PETER KAY

"Women have this weird myth that you can tell the way a guy is in bed by how he is on a dance-floor. That's ludicrous. If a guy's on a dance-floor getting into it and enjoying himself and expressing himself, what does it matter how he is in bed? He's gay."

BILL HICKS

"Men can't say to a woman, 'You aren't fat.' You try, but it never comes out like that. It comes out like: 'You remind me distinctly of a hippo.' Or: 'There is something of the airship about you.' Or: 'I shall call you Rotunda.'"

* FROM THE DVD *ALAN DAVIES: URBAN TRAUMA*

"An Iraqi judge officially dropped all remaining charges against Saddam. That's nice. You don't want to leave a guy hanging."

JAY LENO

"Vodafone say they're the word's largest mobile community. Now, correct me if I'm wrong, but that's the gypsies."

JIMMY CARR

"Nobody ever dares make cup-a-soup in a bowl."

PETER KAY

"Hairdryers are already blowing and yet people wave them like that. What's that for? To get more wind?"

FROM THE DVD *LEE EVANS: LIVE IN SCOTLAND*

"President Bush wants to set up a national database of convicted sex offenders on the internet. Don't we have this already? It's called MySpace."

JAY LENO, US TALKSHOW HOST

"I get broody, like everybody else, but when I do, I set my alarm clock to go off every hour throughout the night, cover all my favourite stuff in snot and jam, and set fire to £500. Then the feeling goes."

JEFF GREEN

"If your surname's 'Dumpty', don't call your first-born 'Humpty'. He probably jumped off that wall."

RICKY GERVAIS

"If you drop a Bible on a field mouse, it'll kill it. So maybe the Bible's not all good after all."

HARRY HILL

"So I was shopping at Ikea and decided to grab a ham sandwich from the kiosk. They gave me two slices of bread, a chunk of ham, an Allen key and told me to construct it myself. It was nice. The key was gritty but went down OK."

DARREN CASEY, MELBOURNE COMEDY FESTIVAL

"You girls would never help us boys out. You'd never undo the top button of your jeans. It was like trying to stroke a dog through a letterbox."

JEFF GREEN FROM THE DVD *BACK FROM THE BEWILDERNESS*

"I had a mate whose dream was to be run over by a steam train. It happened last week. Chuffed to bits, he was."

TIM VINE

"You know when people say they've been abducted by aliens, they always describe them, and it's always the same. A big head and big black eyes. I wonder if, rather than being abducted by aliens, they've actually been abducted by pandas. You've been abducted by pandas... you lie and say aliens! But at night, when darkness falls, the nightmares return... 'No, Chi Chi, nooo! No more bamboo!'"

HARRY HILL FROM FROM THE DVD *FIRST CLASS SCAMP*

"I saw an 'L' key get stuck on a typewriter, started churning out Welsh: or as I prefer to call it, 'code.'"

AL MURRAY

"I got talking to a cab driver the other day. He told me 'I love this job, I'm my own boss, nobody tells me what to do.' I said, 'Left here.'"

JIMMY CARR

'I finally saw The 40 Year Old Virgin. *It was a line of guys waiting for the Playstation 3."*

JAY LENO, US TALKSHOW HOST

"A woman came from the parish council and asked me if I wanted to run a half marathon. And I said, 'Oh no, I couldn't do a half marathon.' And she said, 'You really should think about it. It's for partially sighted and blind children.' So I thought, 'Well, fuck it, I could win that.'"

DAVE SPIKEY

"Fat people say, 'It's glandular.' It's not glandular, is it? It's greed… And how come fat people get the same baggage allowance on flights as everyone else? 'Sorry, no bags. You spent your 50kg on your tits.'"

RICKY GERVAIS

"I think drowning would be a horrible way to die, but maybe a little less horrible if you're really thirsty. That's why when I'm on a boat, I bring a life jacket but also a bag of crisps. If we're going down, I say 'Give me those crisps, I'm going down parched'"

DEMETRI MARTIN, STAND-UP

"I used to think the brain was the greatest organ in the human body. Then I thought, 'Hey! Look what's telling me that!'"

EMO PHILIPS, US STAND-UP

"What's red and sits in the corner? A naughty bus."

DAVID MITCHELL *THAT MITCHELL AND WEBB LOOK*

"There's a lot of controversy over gay people adopting. I would have loved to have a gay dad. Remember all that stuff at school? 'My dad'll batter your dad.' 'No, my dad'll batter your dad.' 'Listen, my dad'll shag *your dad.'"*

FRANKIE BOYLE

"Employee of the month is a good example of how somebody can be both a winner and a loser at the same time."

DEMETRI MARTIN

"I went out the other day, and bought some blond hair and a pair of blue eyes. I'm saving them for the right Caucasian."

TIM VINE

"When the kids in the playground discovered I had a possibly fatal allergy to peanuts, they'd push me up against the wall and make me play Russian roulette with a packet of Revels." Milton Jones

"I got an odd-job man in. He was useless. Gave him a list of eight things to do and he only did numbers one, three, five and seven. Had to get an even-man in to finish it off." STEPHEN GRANT

"I used to go to the playground and watch all the children run and scream... They didn't know I was using blanks."

EMO PHILLIPS

"Christmases were terrible as a poor kid. My sister got a miniature set of perfumes called Ample. Even I could see where my dad had scraped off the 'S'."

STEPHEN K AMOS

"I'd rather see a pregnant girl standing up on a bus, than a fat girl sitting down, crying."

JIMMY CARR

"An air steward at Glasgow Airport set off a security alert after overhearing a man say he was a Basque terrorist. Turns out it was Adam Clayton from U2. He said he was a bass guitarist."

TAM COWAN, DAILY RECORD

"The worst time to have a heart attack is during a game of charades. Especially if the other players are bad guessers. 'Fat Guy On The Floor? I've never seen THAT movie.'"

Demetri Martin

"So I said to my personal trainer 'Can you teach me to do the splits?'
He said 'How flexible are you?'
I said 'I can't make Tuesdays'.

PETER KAY

"So I rang up a local building firm and said, 'I want a skip outside my house.' He said, 'I'm not stopping you.'"

TIM VINE

"Steven Hawking's not a genius. He's pretentious. Born in Kent and talks with an American accent."

RICKY GERVAIS

"I used to go jogging. I went four miles a day. I did it for two weeks. I got so fucking far away from my house I couldn't get back."

LEE EVANS

"When I was a kid, I asked my mother: 'Mum, what's a transvestite?'
She said, 'That's your father, I'm over here.'"

ADRIAN POYNTON, STAND-UP

"The average American car weighs 500lbs more than it did 10 years ago. Of course, that's only true if the average American is sitting in it."

CONAN O'BRIEN, US CHAT SHOW HOST

"My pyjamas have pockets. They're really useful, because now I don't have to carry stuff while I sleep."

DEMETRI MARTIN, US STAND-UP

"If we didn't have rules, where would we be? France."

AL MURRAY

"If guys could blow themselves, then ladies, you'd be alone in this room right now. Watching an empty stage."

BILL HICKS

"Why do builders have see-through lunchboxes? So they can tell if they're going home or coming to work."

JACK DEE

"Fat people make excuses. They say, 'I eat the occasional sweet.' Yeah, three-piece suite."

RICKY GERVAIS

"Health experts reckon laughing for 15 minutes a day could win the war against obesity. So now you know why Dawn French (aka Mrs Lenny Henry) is the size of a No.67 bus."

TAM COWAN, *THE DAILY RECORD*

"A young man having sex with an old woman is advised to treat the experience like rock climbing: stare at the craggy face and try not to glance at the horrors, beneath."

GARRY BUSHELL, DAILY STAR

"Have you noticed the way that burns victims stick together?"

CAREY RX

"I went to Wales. No bugger talks to you. I know how Kevin Costner felt in *Dances With Wolves*. Six weeks on a beach, on my own, sitting there, being feared by the locals. Until eventually they brought me a bit of bread. And I befriended them and I started to live as one of them and for the first time in my life I was happy. And I thought, 'Why bother doing this stand-up shit when I can be here and be loved for who I am.' And I'd have stayed there. But I made the fatal mistake of buying some Coco Pops. Which, I don't know if you know, turn the milk brown. I was nearly burnt as a fucking witch. I'm sitting there eating me breakfast and they're building a wicker man in the back garden. I had to flee for me life dressed a sheep. Do you know how hard it is making a credible sheep noise while some fucker's taking you roughly from behind? 'BAAAAAA!' I broke down, I couldn't help it. 'Could you be more gentle!' Farmer shat himself. I was dragged back to the village as a local oddity. Everyone's going, 'I don't see what's so special about him.' Farmer's going, 'Wait till you fuck him – he talks!' I spent six weeks tied up in the village square, with every dozy bastard having a go at me... [Makes pelvis-thrusting motions] 'Come on, tell me fortune.' 'You'll never marry...'"

FROM THE JOHNNY VEGAS DVD *WHO'S READY FOR ICE CREAM?*

"You know the world is going crazy when the best rapper is white, the best golfer is black, the tallest guy in the NBA is Chinese, the Swiss hold the America's Cup, France is accusing the US of arrogance, Germany doesn't want to go to war and the three most powerful men in America are named Bush, Dick, and Colon."

CHRIS ROCK

"This is absolutely fantastic – it's better than sex!"

JOCKEY ROBBIE POWER AFTER WINNING THE GRAND NATIONAL ON SILVER BIRCH

"You might get some now, then!"

TRAINER GORDON ELLIOTT'S INSTANT REPLY

"I broke the legs of four players and a couple of arms… And that was just our team in training."

NO WONDER BRIT BOXER DAVID "HAYEMAKER" HAYE WAS BANNED FROM SCHOOL FOOTBALL

"I used to milk 100 cows, six days a week, and then go out to a place like Newbridge in Wales on a wet Wednesday night and have my head kicked in. And do you know what? I miss those days."

England rugby union player Phil Vickery looks back on his time as a farmer and amateur player

It's the last game of the 2003/04 season, and Martin Keown needs just one more appearance to collect his Premiership winner's medal. With one minute to go, Arsenal subs, Keown and Parlour are warming up when Wengers signals for his their and final substitution. "Ray," shouts Pat Rice, "get stripped off." Keown, at this point – his last chance of silverwear disappearing over the horizon faster than a Beckham penalty – understandably goes ballistic, only to find the whole Arsenal bench laughing and pointing at him. He was going to be subbed on all the time! The japes!

Gazza's first training session after his £5million move to Lazio – and career threatening knee knack – had just about every journalist in Italy on the sidelines. After a couple of gentle laps of the pitch, Gazza fell to the floor, clutching his dodgy knee, screaming in agony and writhing around on the floor. A deathly silence spread over the training ground as the club's physios sprinted to the stricken Geordie. When the medics were a few yards away, Gazza stood up and carried on jogging round the pitch without saying a word…

"If I'm looking good, it'll give me that extra edge. It's all part of the routine – shaving my legs, putting on fake tan and doing my hair."

GAVIN HENSON'S CAMP PRE-MATCH GROOMING RITUAL

The old 'is that a lump of shit in your hand or are you just pleased to see me' trick, as described by Razor Ruddock: "Steve Sedgley came up and shook my hand to wish me well before a match. It wasn't until I'd run on the pitch that I realised my hand was caked in shit. It stunk and I had to spend the rest of the half trying to get it off." This from a man who used to piss his pants to warm himself up on a cold day...

"I'd say about 50 per cent of the squads I'm in these days shave their legs and use fake tan"

GAVIN HENSON ENDEARS HIMSELF EVEN

"They remind me a bit of Laurel and Hardy, er, in that they are different characters who complement each other nicely."

Shane Warne on Flintoff and Strauss

"Stan Collymore once got beaten up by big rugby players. They say Stan was bragging about having a fight with a rugby player outside a pub and giving him a good hiding. But he didn't say that at all. What he actually said was the last time he was in a car park, he splattered on Austin Healey."
Frank Skinner

When Faustino Asprilla arrived in Newcastle, he was desperate to find out what was hip and trendy in the UK at the time. So the squad marched the Colombian striker straight down to Newcastle's hottest clothing emporium – the local Disney store – and kitted him out with a natty Daffy Duck waistcoat and tie combo. Tino could never understand the funny looks he got when he was 'out' on the 'toon'.

"Well, it makes it more pleasant to look at you in your thin T-shirt."

David Coulthard's response to ITV reporter Louise Goodman asking how the cold weather would affect his driving

"America's favourite pastime starts again. It's that season again when big sweaty guys start grabbing their crotches, yelling and swinging baseball bats – yes, *The Sopranos* is back."

Craig Ferguson, US talkshow host

"If your parents are getting divorced, it can be a very traumatic time. Don't worry: it's not your fault. Your mum's a slag."

JIMMY CARR, 8 *OUT OF 10 CATS*

"Did you know that 60 per cent of all cosmetic surgery patients are disappointed with the results? Though they look pleasantly surprised."

Jimmy Carr, 8 *Out of 10 Cats*

A new study shows that eating salmon is not only good for you, but makes you happier. However, some experts disagree: grizzly bears.

Saturday Night Live

"George Bush is now also worried about global warming, but he has a plan. He's going to invade the sun."

David Letterman, The Late Show

"The Government is worried about the growing number of people subscribing to suicide websites. Subscribing? Surely it's cheaper to pay as you go?"

ALAN CARR, *THE FRIDAY NIGHT PROJECT*

"Muse's equipment was destroyed by high winds at the aptly-named Hurricane Festival in Germany recently. I can only wish them the best of luck when they play at this year's World AIDS Day."

Simon Amstell , *Never Mind The Buzzcocks*

"A guy walks into a dentist's office and says, 'I think I'm a moth.' The dentist says, 'Well, if you think you're a moth, why did you come to the dentist's office?' The guy says, 'Well, the light was on.'"

JD, Scrubs

SOUTH PARK QUOTES:

Cartman *(after a goat is sent to him)*: *It's an Afghanistan goat, so it can't stay here, or else it'll choke on the sweet air of freedom.*

Wendy: *Dude, dolphins are intelligent and friendly!*
Cartman: *If they're so smart, how come they live in igloos? Intelligent and friendly on rye bread with mayo please.*

Cartman: *Independent films are those black and white hippy movies. They're always about gay cowboys eating pudding.*

Kyle: *Wow, that's a lot of semen Cartman.*
Cartman: *Yeah. I got it from this guy Ralph in an alley. And the sweet thing is, the stupid asshole didn't even charge me money for it. He just made me close my eyes and suck it out of a hose.*

Kyle: *I hate being small and Jewish. I feel like a tall black man.*
Plastic surgeon: *You need a negroplasty. It's a fairly common procedure. Just the reverse of a caucasioplasty like Michael Jackson had.*

Paris Hilton: *I'm pleased to be here in Douth Dark to open my brand new store. A store where girls can buy everything they need to be just like me: Stupid Spoiled Whore.*

Mr Garrison: *Now does anyone know what sexual harassment means? Yes, Eric?*
Cartman: *When you're trying to have intercourse with a lady friend and some other guy comes up and tickles your balls from behind.*

SEINFELD QUOTES:

Jerry: *Looking at cleavage is like looking at the sun. You don't stare at it. It's too risky. You get a sense of it and then you look away.*

George *[on dating a woman in jail]: Jerry, I like being with her. Plus, I know where she is all the time. I have relatively no competition. And you know how you live in fear of the pop-in? No "in the neighbourhood," no "I saw your light was on."*

George: *She calls me up at my office, she says, "We have to talk."*
Jerry: *Ugh, the four worst words in the English language.*
George: That, or "Whose bra is this?"

George: *Who buys an umbrella anyway? You can get them for free at the coffee shop, by the door in those metal cans.*
Jerry: *Those belong to people.*

George: *Why go to funerals? You think dead people care who's at the funeral? They don't even know they're having a funeral. It's not like she's hanging out in the back going, "I can't believe Jerry didn't show up".*
Elaine: *Maybe she's there in spirit.*
George: *If you're a spirit, and you can travel to other dimensions and galaxies, and find out the mysteries of the universe, you think you'll want to hang around Drexler's funeral home on Ocean Parkway?*

Jerry: *Breaking up is like knocking over a Coke machine. You can't do it in one push, you got to rock it back and forth a few times, and then it goes over.*

FAMILY GUY QUOTES:

Chris: *Dad, what's the whale's blowhole for?*
Peter: *I'll tell you what it's not for, son. And when I do, you'll understand why I can never go back to Sea World.*

Peter: *OK, here's another riddle. A woman has two children. A psycho killer tells her she can only keep one. Which one does she let him kill?*
Brian: *That's not a riddle. That's just terrible.*
Peter: *Wrong, the ugly one!*

Brian: *Who the hell buys a novelty fire extinguisher?*
Peter: *I'll tell you who. Someone who cares enough about physical comedy to put his whole family at risk.*

Lois, *watching a sexy beer ad*: *I guarantee you a man made that commercial.*
Peter: *Of course a man made it. It's a commercial, Lois, not a delicious thanksgiving dinner.*

Lois: *I care about the size of your penis as much as you care about the size of my breasts.*
Peter: *Oh my God! (runs off crying)*

Stewie, *to a prostitute*: *So, is there any tread left on the tyres? Or would it be like throwing a hotdog down a hallway?*

Lois: *Honey, what do you say we uh… christen these new sheets, huh?*
Peter: *Why Lois Griffin, you naughty girl.*
Lois: *Hehehe… that's me.*

Peter: *You dirty hustler.*
Lois: *Hehehehe...*
Peter: *You filthy, stinky prostitute.*
Lois: *Aha, ok I get it...*
Peter: *You foul, venereal disease carrying, street walking whore.*
Lois: *Alright, that's enough!*

FUTURAMA QUOTES:

Amy Wong: *You just have to give guys a chance. Sometimes you meet a guy and think he's a pig, but then later on you realize he actually has a really good body.*

Soldier: *This is the worst part. The calm before the battle.*
Fry: *And then the battle is not so bad?*
Soldier: *Oh, right. I forgot about the battle.*

Fry: *Man, I thought Ultimate Robot Fighting was real, like pro wrestling, but it turns out it's fixed, like boxing.*

Oscar Presenter: *And the nominees for Best Soft Drink Product Placement are...* Star Trek: The Pepsi Generation, They Call Me Mr. Pibb, *and* Snow White and the Seven-ups.

Nibblonian: *You are the last hope of the universe.*
Fry: *So I really am important? How I feel when I'm drunk is correct?*
Nibblonian: *Yes – except the Dave Matthews Band doesn't rock.*

Bender: *You're watching* Futurama, *the show that doesn't condone the cool crime of robbery.*

Captain Zapp Brannigan: *If we hit that bullseye, the rest of the dominoes should fall like a house of cards. Checkmate.*

THE SIMPSONS QUOTES:

Chief Wiggum: *No, you have the wrong number. This is 91… 2.*

Ralph Wiggum: *Me fail English? That's unpossible!*

Homer to Bart: *These three little sentences will get you through life.*
'Oh good idea boss!' 'Cover for me'. 'It was like that when I got here.'

Scully from the X-Files: *This is a simple lie detector test. I'll ask you a few yes-or-no questions and you just answer truthfully. Do you understand?*
Homer: *Yes. (Lie detector explodes).*

Homer: *I saw this movie about a bus that had to* speed *around the city, keeping its* speed *over fifty. And if its* speed *dropped, the bus would explode. I think it was called…* The Bus That Couldn't Slow Down.

Mr Burns: *Oh, so Mother Nature needs a favour? Well, maybe she should have thought of that when she was besetting us with droughts and floods and poison monkeys.*

Homer: *Every time I learn something new it pushes some old stuff outta my brain. Remember when I took that wine tasting lesson and I forgot how to drive?*

Homer: *Maybe, just once, someone will call me 'sir' without adding, 'you're making a scene.'*

Homer *(pointing at Uruguay on a globe)*: *'Look at this country: U R Gay'.*

Marge *(on radio)*: *Husband on murderous rampage. Send help. Over.*
Chief Wiggum: *Phew, thank God it's over. I was worried for a little bit.*

Mr Burns: *You'd kneel before me, wouldn't you Smithers?*
Smithers: Boy, would I.

ZOO

SPORTS JOKES

Because football's a funny old game. And so are the rest of them.

"Steve Waugh – I reckon he'd sledge his own kids in a game of backyard cricket. He'd say: 'I had sex with your mother last night!'"
Will Anderson

Sophie Ellis Bextor has been found headbutted to death in the apartment of a French footballer. Apparently it was murder on Zidane's floor!

"There's always one of my uncles who watches a boxing match with me and says 'Sure. Ten million dollars. You know, for that kind of money, I'd fight him.' As if someone is going to pay $200 a ticket to see a 57-year-old carpet salesman get hit in the face once and cry."
Larry Miller

"A new survey says over half of sick days are claimed falsely – and many of these fake sickies coincide with sporting events. For example, a lot of people failed to turn up during the Cricket World Cup. Half the England team, for example."
Steve Punt, The Now Show

Manchester United Viruses...

The Manchester United Fan Virus – your computer develops a memory disorder and forgets about everything before 1993.

The Manchester United Shirt Virus – This one is especially hard to detect as it changes format every three months.

The Alex Ferguson Virus – The computer develops a continuous whining noise. The on screen clock runs slower than all the other computers in the building.

The Tim Howard Virus – The computer looks like it's functioning normally but you can't save anything.

"Britain was battered by torrential storms this week; hundreds of people have fled Wolverhampton. It wasn't raining but they found an old bus and saw an opportunity for a better life. Meanwhile, Tim Henman is thinking about getting into coaching... offering discount fares to all of Britain's market towns."

JIMMY CARR, *8 OUT OF 10 CATS*

Name three English football teams with a swear-word in their name.

Arsenal, Scunthorpe and fucking Chelsea.

Why did the Gers fan *never* cross the road?
He was waiting for the Green Man to turn Orange.

St James' Park was broken into last night and the entire contents of the trophy room were stolen. Newcastle police are believed to be looking for a man with a black and white carpet.

"Sport: essentially just enormous fat people sat down, stuffing their faces, roaring their disapproval at the most finely-tuned athletes in the world."

DYLAN MORAN

"I was shocked by David Pleat's slanderous comments about the Man United Wags during this week's win. Especially his accusation that 'Smith's chance was even easier than Saha's missus'."
Off The Fiver

"Me and about eight mates went up Chelsea last week. Bill Clinton was fucking furious."

FRANK SKINNER

Two Irishmen are fishing. The first reels in his line and sees that he's snagged an old bottle. As he's taking it off the hook, a genie pops out and promises to grant him one wish. "Turn the lake into beer," he says. The genie goes "Poof!" and the lake turns into beer.
Second Irishman says, "You jerk. Now we've got to piss in the boat."

What does Cheryl Tweedy get when she offers Ashley Cole a penny for his thoughts?
Change

Two blokes are walking through a cemetery when they happen upon a tombstone that reads: 'Here lies John Sweeney, a good man and a Chelsea fan.' One of the men turns to the other and asks, "When the hell did they start putting two people in one grave?"

Man City have a new line of cologne. It's a little different though; you wear it and the other guy scores.

WHAT'S THE DIFFERENCE BETWEEN KEIRON DYER AND A COMPUTER?
YOU ONLY HAVE TO PUNCH INFORMATION INTO A COMPUTER ONCE.

What would you get if Man U were relegated?
45,000 more Chelsea fans.

You see a Liverpool fan on a bike – why shouldn't you swerve to hit him?
It might be your bike.

Rafa Benitez sent scouts out around the world looking for a new striker to lead the Liverpool forward line.

One of the scouts tells him about a promising young Iraqi. Rafa flies to Baghdad to watch him, is suitably impressed, buys him and brings him back to Anfield.

Two weeks later Liverpool are 4-0 down to Man United with only 20 minutes left. Rafa gives the young Iraqi striker the nod and brings him on. The lad is a sensation, scores five in 20 minutes and wins the game for Liverpool. The fans love him and everyone hails him as the next superstar.

When he's done his interviews and signed autographs, the lad phones his mum to tell her about his English football debut. "Hello mum, guess what?" he says. "We were 4-0 down but I scored five in 20 minutes and we won. Everybody loves me, the fans, the media, they all love me".

"Wonderful," says his mum. "Let me tell you about my day. Your father got shot in the street, your sister and I were ambushed and beaten and your brother has joined a gang of looters while you were having a great time."

With this news, the young lad is very upset. "What can I say mum, except I'm so sorry".

"Sorry?" exclaims his mum. "It's your fault we all moved to Liverpool in the first fucking place."

In a small town in Northern Ireland, the local Catholic team were about to take the field against the local Protestants. "Remember, lads," said the coach, "if you can't kick the ball, kick the player's shins, and if you can't kick his shins, trip him and kick his head. Now, as soon as we find the ball we'll kick off."
"Fuck the ball," said a voice from the back. "Let's get on with the game."

What's the difference between OJ Simpson and Newcastle?

OJ HAS A MORE CREDIBLE DEFENCE

What's the difference between a Gillingham fan and a coconut?

One's thick and hairy, the other's a tropical nut.

What's the difference between Jose Mourinho and God?
God doesn't think he's Jose Mourinho.

"At Wimbledon Henman has Henman Hill named after him, Murray has Murray Mound and Greg [Rusedski] has a bakers opposite the station."
JIMMY CARR, *8 OUT OF 10 CATS*

The fire brigade phones Martin Jol in the early hours of Sunday morning... "Mr Jol sir, White Hart Lane is on fire!"
"The cups man! Save the cups!" replies Jol.
"Uh, the fire hasn't spread to the canteen yet, sir."

They say that hooliganism and racism are bad, but personally, we think Iain Dowie is the unacceptable face of British football.

What's the difference between Coventry City and the Bermuda triangle?
The Bermuda triangle has three points.

There's a rumour that after the current sponsorship expires, Forest have lined up a new sponsor – Tampax.

The board thought it was appropriate as the club is going through a very bad period.

ACCIDENTAL PORN

JUICY MELON

SMEGG PLANT

DROPPING IN AND HANGING OUT

CRISPY TREAT

MAGIC EXPLOSION

FETCH THE TOWEL

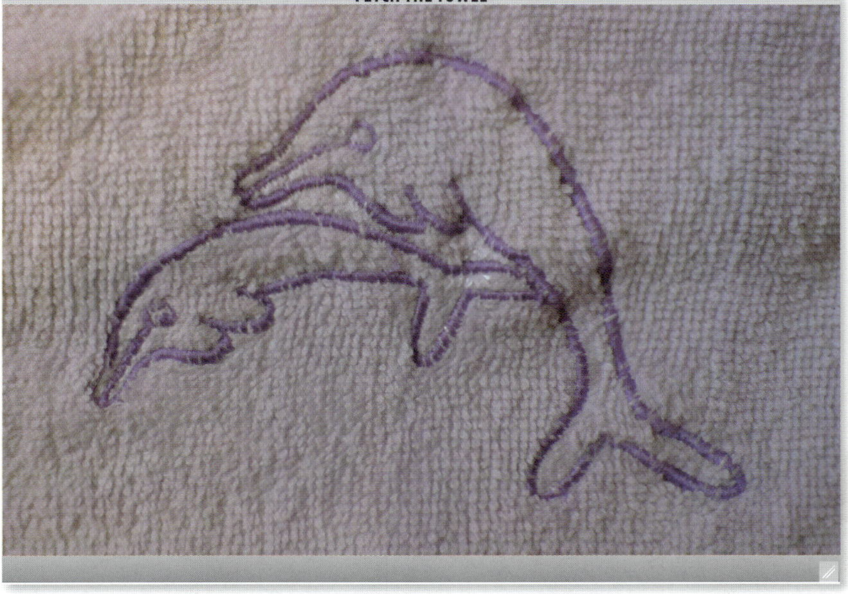

GET YOUR LEGO-VER

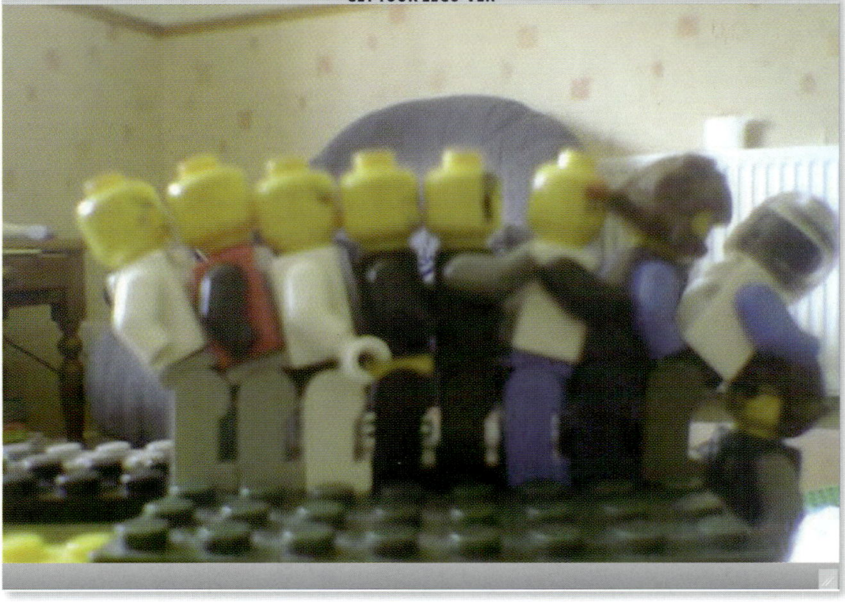

LUCKY PIG

CYBER-LOVE

MAN'S BEST FRIEND

SURPRISED OCTOPUS

ANIMAL FARM

CLEAN FORCES

NOT A GAME

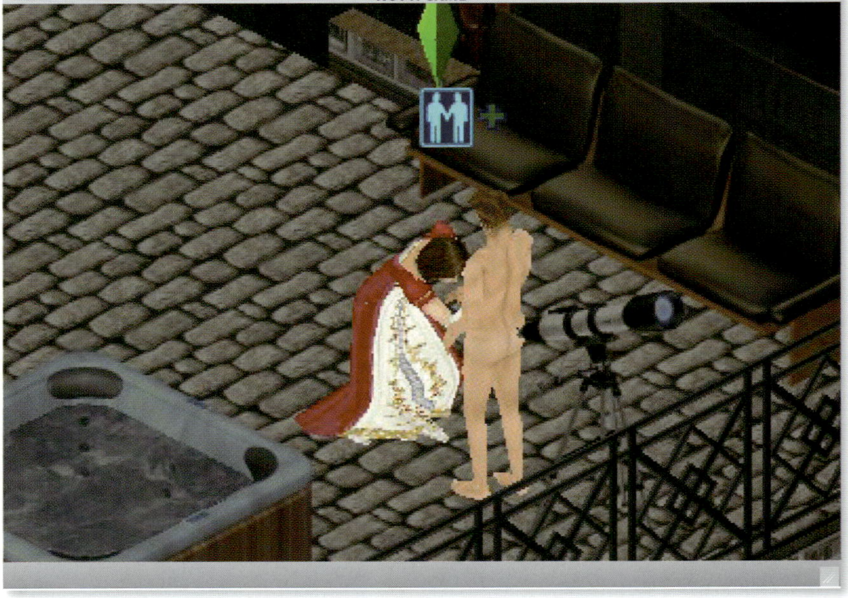

WHAT A RIDE

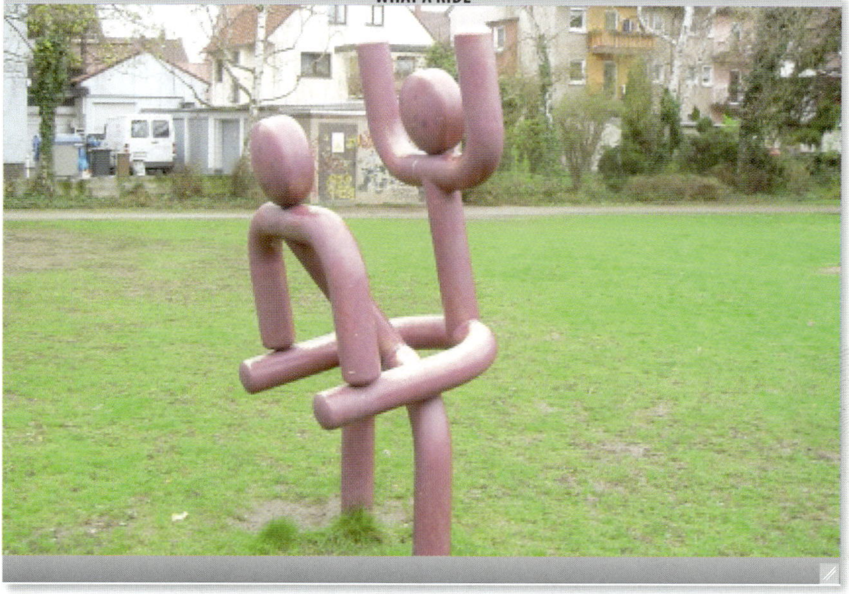

PRIVATE HEALTHCARE

WHAT A JOURNEY

DAILY BREAD

A guy comes home from golfing, and his wife asks him how it went.
"Well, we were doing fine until Bob had a heart attack and died on the fourth hole..."
"Oh my god, that's terrible!"
"You're telling me. For the rest of the afternoon, it was swing, drag Bob, swing, drag Bob..."

A man desperate at Charlton's situation decides to top himself. In his living room, alone, he prepares to hang himself. At the very last moment, he decides upon wearing his full Charlton kit as his last statement. A neighbour, catching sight of the impending incident, informs the police. On arrival, the police quickly remove the Charlton kit and dress the man in stockings and suspenders. The man, totally confused asks why. The policeman simply replies, "It's to avoid embarrassing your family."

Ronaldo goes into Burger King and says "Give me two whoppers".
The cashier says: "Ok, You're not fat and you haven't lost it."

How does Craig Bellamy change a lightbulb?

He holds it in the air, and the world revolves around him.

Pat, a Man United fan, is appearing on *Who Wants To Be A Millionaire*, and he's faced with the £125,000 question. "On the screen is a photograph of a former Manchester United player as a small baby," says Tarrant. "The question is – which player is it?"

"I think it's David Beckham," says Pat, "but I'll phone my friend Mick just to make sure."

They phone Mick, another United supporter, but he's not so sure. "I think it's Peter Schmeichel," he says.

"Are you sure now Mick," says Pat, "I'm convinced it's David Beckham…"

"Definitely," replies Mick.

Pat gives Chris his answer, and after the usual faffing about, finally says, "Sorry Pat, Peter Schmeichel is the wrong answer."

"Oh well," says Pat, "but would you mind telling me who it was?"

"No problem Pat," says Chris, "it was Andy Cole."

How many Manchester City fans does it take to change a light bulb?
None – they're quite happy living in the shadows.

Michael Owen walks into a club and sees a hot woman.
"Get your coat, love," says the striker, "you're coming home with me."
She looks at him and replies: "My, you're a little forward!"

"I backed a horse today, at 20 to 1. It came in at 20 past 4."

Tommy Cooper

How can you tell when Leeds are losing?
It's five past three.

Why won't Crag Bellamy play cricket?
Because he really hates bouncers.

What do you get if you cross the English cricket union team with an Oxo cube?
A laughing stock.

The Sultan of Brunei wanted to give his three favourite sons a Christmas present, so he asked each one what he wanted. The first said he wanted a car, so he gave him Rolls Royce Motors.
The second said he'd like a plane, so he gave him British Aerospace.
The third, and youngest, said he'd like a Mickey Mouse outfit, so he gave him Middlesbrough.

A Man United fan, about 8 years old, goes into a sports shop to buy a United football. It's £25 but the boy only has £5, so he says to the shopkeeper, "Blindfold me and pick any football off that shelf and I bet I can guess what football team is on the ball. If I get it right you have to give me the United ball."
So he blindfolds the boy, gets the ball off the shelf and puts it in front of the boy's face. The boy shouts, "It's Wolves! – I can hear the sound of a pack of wolves in the woods." So the shopkeeper gets a ball from the shelf puts it in front of the boy's face. The boy shouts, "It's Arsenal! I can hear the guns on a bloody war field."
The shocked shopkeeper says, "Right, get this one and you can have the ball and the Beckham boots." So he gets the ball puts it in front of the boy's face. The boy shouts "It's Palace."
"How did you get that one?" says the shopkeeper.
The boy says, "Well, it's going down."

Thierry Henry, Ronaldinho and Beckham are at the pearly gates of heaven. St. Peter opens the gate, turns to Henry and asks "Why do you deserve eternal happiness in Heaven my son?"

Thierry replies "I am an artist; I inspire young people to be great footballers, and in turn take them away from a life of crime." St. Peter nods, impressed.

He turns to Ronaldinho and asks the same question. Ronnie retorts "When I play football I treat everyone as an equal, I see no ethnic or racial divides. The street urchin from Rio is the same as the superstar from Barcelona." Once again St. Peter is impressed and nods. Next he turns to Beckham and says: "I suppose you are looking for your ball back?"

How many Fulham supporters does it take to unscrew a lightbulb? Both of them.

*Top tip for Manchester United fans:
don't waste money on expensive new kits every season. Simply strap a large inflatable penis to your forehead, and everyone will immediately know which team you support.*

What do you call an England cricketer with 100 runs against his name?
A bowler.

What does General Pinochet and Blackburn Rovers have in common?
They both round people up in football stadiums and torture them.

Three old football fans are in a church, praying for their teams. The first one asks, "Oh Lord, when will England next win the World Cup?" God replies, "In the next five years"
"But I'll be dead by then", says the man.
The second one asks, "Oh Lord, when will Man United next win the European Cup?"
The Good Lord answers, "In the next ten years".
"But I'll be dead by then", says the man.
The third one asks, "Oh Lord, when will Tottenham win the Premiership?"
God answers, "I'll be dead by then!"

One day, a Spurs fan was walking along the beach and came across an odd-looking bottle. Not being one to ignore tradition, he rubbed it and, much to his surprise, a Genie actually appeared. "For releasing me from the bottle, I will grant you three wishes," said the Genie. The man was ecstatic. "But there's a catch," the Genie continued. "For each of your wishes, every Arsenal supporter in the world will receive double what you asked for."

"Hey, I can live with that! No problem!" replied the elated man. "What is your first wish?" asked the Genie. "Well, I've always wanted a Ferrari!" Poof ! A Ferrari appeared in front of the man. "Now, every Gooner in the world has been given two Ferraris," said the Genie. "What is your next wish?" "I could really use a million dollars..." replied the man, and Poof! One million dollars appeared at his feet. "Now, every Gooner in the world is two million dollars richer," the Genie reminded the man. "Well, that's okay, as long as I've got my million," replied the Spurs fan. "And what is your final wish?" asked the Genie. The man thought long and hard, and finally said, "Well, you know, I've always wanted to donate a kidney..."

Why do people take an instant dislike to Robbie Savage?

It just saves time.

Brazil are due to play Scotland when, five minutes before the game, Ronaldo goes into the Brazilian changing room to find all his teammates looking a bit glum.
"What's up?" he asks.
"Well, we're having trouble getting motivated for this game. We know it's important but it's only Scotland. They're shite and we can't be bothered," replies Ronaldinho.
Ronaldo looks at them and says "Well, I reckon I can beat these by myself, you lads go down the pub."
So Ronaldo goes out to play Scotland by himself and the rest of the Brazilian team go off for a few jars.
After a few pints they ask the landlord to put teletext on. A big cheer goes up as the screen reads "Scotland 0 Brazil 1 (Ronaldo 10 minutes)". He's beating Scotland all by himself!
A few pints later and the game is forgotten until someone remembers "It must be full time now, let's see how he got on". They put teletext on:
"Final score: Scotland 1 (Dickov 89 minutes) Brazil 1 (Ronaldo 10 minutes)".
They can't believe it, he's single-handedly got a draw against Scotland! They rush back to the stadium to congratulate him and find him in the dressing room with his head in his hands.
Kaka says, "You got a draw against Scotland, all by yourself. And they only scored at the very, very end! That's amazing."
"No, No, I have let you down," replies Ronaldo. "I got sent off after 12 minutes."

One morning, a foursome of men are waiting at the men's tee, while a foursome of ladies are hitting from the ladies' tee.
The ladies really take their time, but finally the last woman is ready to tee off. She hacks it about ten feet, curses, walks over to the ball and hacks it to another ten feet or so. She looks up at the watching men, shrugs and says, "I guess all those f*ing lessons I took this winter didn't help."**
One of the men replies, "Now, there's your problem. You should've taken golf lessons instead. But do you fancy a drink?"

Stamford Bridge has arguably the best pitch in the Premiership these days.
Not entirely surprising, considering all the shit that's been on there in the past.

A Man City and Man United fan collide in a huge accident on the motorway. Both cars are a wreck, but both men are unhurt.
"This must be a sign from God that we are meant to be friends" says the City fan.
"I agree" replies the United fan.
The City fan then returns to the wreckage of his car, and finds a bottle of whiskey he had been saving. "Look" he says to the United fan, "this must be another sign from God, we should drink this whiskey to celebrate our friendship and survival."
He hands the bottle over to the United fan who takes several large gulps from the bottle before passing it back to the City fan, who then puts the top back on & returns the bottle to his car.
"Aren't you having any?" asks the United fan.
"No" replied the City fan, "I think I'll wait 'til the police get here."

Hours after the end of the world, a border dispute emerged between Heaven and Hell. God invited the Devil over to discuss how to resolve the dispute. Satan suggests a game of football between Heaven and Hell.

God, always fair, says to the devil, "the heat must be affecting your brain, the game will be so one sided! Don't you know all the good players go to heaven?"

"Yeah," replied the Devil, smiling, "but we've got all the refs..."

Top Ten Hybrid Animals

Two become one. Simple. Sometimes scary

1 TIGON/LIGER That's a male tiger/ female lion (tigon) and vice versa for a liger. Liger's are the world's largest cats, with some standing 12ft tall on their hind legs and weigh around half a ton.

2 WOLF DOG Dogs and wolves crossbreed freely, and this is the result. The jaws are stronger than a dog, but they can still be domesticated and obedience trained.

3 IRON AGE PIG Domestic Tamworth pigs crossed with wild boars. Tamer than boars, but still bred only for specialist pork sausages.

4 ZEBROID The general term for zebra crosses. Specifically, a zorse is zebra/ horse, a zonkey is zebra/donkey and a zony crosses zebra with pony.

5 CAMA Camel and a llama. Born via artificial insemination due to the size difference. Sadly, the hump gets lost on the process.

6 GROLAR/PIZZLY When polar bears and grizzlies meet and do sex. The bears are genetically similar, but tend to avoid each other in the wild. In April 2006 a hunter managed to shoot one in Canada. So while we know they exist, we blew away the only one that came close.

7 LEOPON The bastard child of a male leopard and female lion. They like to "climb and enjoy water". A successful breeding program exists in Japan.

8 HYBRID PHEASANT The colourful result of a golden pheasant crossed with a lady Amherst's pheasant.

9 WOLPHIN Take a bottlenose dolphin and a killer whale and let them at it. This is the result. Currently there are just two in captivity, in Hawaii's Sea Life Park.

10 TI-LIGER, TI-TIGON, LI-TIGON, LI-LIGER The ultimate! A hybrid among hybrids. Crossbreeding between male tiger and female liger/tigon or male lion with female tigon/ liger. Only a few examples exist in specialist research facilities.

Top Ten Most Promiscuous Nations by the Amount of Times People Have Sex a Year

1. Greece 138
2. Croatia 134
3. Serbia & Montenegro 128
4. Bulgaria 127
5. Czech Republic 120 = France 120
7. United Kingdom 118
8 Netherlands 115 = Poland 115
10 United States 114

(www.durex.com)

Top Ten Most Expensive Bits of Football Memorabilia

1 The FA Challenge Cup (1896–1910)
£478,400

2 Jules Rimet replica trophy
£254,000

3 Alan Ball's 1966 World Cup Winner's medal 2005
£164,800

4 Pele's shirt from the 1970 World Cup Final 2002
£157,750

5 Part of ex-Wolves and England captain Billy Wright's medal collection 1996
£134,550

6 Gordon Banks 1966 World Cup Winner's medal 2001
£124,750

7 Collection of medals, caps and shirts awarded to Ray Kennedy 1993
£101,200

8 Geoff Hurst's red shirt from the 1966 World Cup Final 2001
£91,750

9 Ray Wilson's 1966 World Cup Winner's medal 2002
£80,750

10 Pele's shirt from the 1958 World Cup Final 2004
£70,505

Top 10 UK Fetishes

1. Leather/rubber/latex/vinyl
2. Feet/hands
3. Domination/submission
4. Stomachs
5. Body piercing
6. Fingernails/lipstick
7. Braids/ponytails/pigtails
8. Water
9. Voyeurism/exhibitionism
10. Golden Showers

TOP TEN LAST WORDS

1 "I should never have switched from Scotch to Martinis."
Humphrey Bogart (1899–1957)

2 "These curtains are killing me; one of us has got to go."
Oscar Wilde (1854–1900)

3 "Adieu, mes amis, je vais à la gloire!" (Farewell my friends, I go to glory!)
Isadora Duncan (1877–1927)

4 "Damn it... Don't you dare ask God to help me."
Joan Crawford (1905–77) to her maid as she began to pray

5 "Hurry up, you Hoosier bastard; I could kill ten men while you're fooling around!"
Carl Panzram (1891–1930) prior to his execution

6 "Don't let it end like this. Tell them I said something."
Pancho Villa (1878–1923)

7 "I did not know that we had ever quarreled."
Henry David Thoreau (1817–62) when urged to make peace with God

8 "I'm warning you boys, I'm a screamer."
Davy Crockett (1786–1836), prior to his execution

9 "Now, now, my good man, this is no time for making enemies."
Voltaire (1694–1778), when asked to renounce Satan

10 "Thank God. I'm tired of being the funniest person in the room."
Del Close (1934–99) *Source: www.askmen.com*

TOP TEN MOST PROLIFIC 'SWORDSMEN'

1. Umberto Billo (Venetian hotel porter) – 8,000
2. Charlie Sheen (actor) – 5,000
3. Gene Simmons (KISS frontman) – 4,600
4. Julio Iglesias (singer) – 3,000
= Engelbert Humperdink (singer) – 3,000
6. Ilie Nastase
7. Jack Nicholson (actor) – 2,000
8. Lemmy Kilmister (Motorhead frontman) – 1,200
9. Earvin 'Magic' Johnson (basketball star) – 1,000
= Bill Wyman (ex-Rolling Stone) – 1,000

Top Ten Names & Bra-Sizes of 'Big Boob Superstars'

1. Chelsea Charms 153XXX
2. Cindy Fulsome 120QQQ
3. Plenty Uptopp 127PPP
4. Maxi Mounds 42M
5. Minka 44KK
6. Traci Topps 34JJ
7. B.B. Gunns 76HHH
8. Pandora Peaks 72HHH
9. Crystal Gunns 46GG
10. Donita Dunes 44GG

Top Ten Oldest Scottish Distilleries

1 Glenturret 1775
2 Bowmore 1779
3 Strathisla 1786
4 Tobermory 1795
5= Highland Park 1798
5= Ardbeg 1798
5= Glen Garioch 1798
8 Glenburgie 1810
9 Laphroaig 1816
10= Lagavulin 1817
10= Teaninich 1817

TOP TEN STRONGEST BEERS EVER BREWED

1. Hair Of The Dog Dave, USA 29% ABV

2. Hakusekikan Eisbock, Japan 28%

3. Samuel Adams Utopias, USA 25%

4. Barley John's Rosie's Ale, USA 23%

5. Dogfish Head World Wide Stout, USA 22%

6. Dogfish Head 120 Minute IPA, USA 21%

7. Grand Lake Holy Grail, USA 20%

8. Samuel Adams Millennium, USA 19.5%

9. Dogfish Head Raison d'Extra, USA 18.5%

10. Dogfish Head Fort, USA 18%

TOP 10 BEST URINALS IN THE WORLD (AND BEYOND)

1 Amundsen-Scott South Pole Station, South Pole, Antarctica
2 The Taj Mahal, Agra, Uttar Pradesh, India
3 Nature's Call by Clark Sorensen, San Francisco, USA
4 Public Rest Rooms of Rothesay, Rothesay, Isle of Bute, UK
5 Mystique Night Club – Kisses, Bangkok, Thailand
6 Women's Urinal at Dairy Queen, Port Charlotte, Florida, USA
7 Stockholm-Arlanda Airport, Stockholm, Sweden
8 International Space Station, In Space
9 John Michael Kohler Arts Center, New York, USA
10 The Felix, Hong Kong

Source: www.urinal.net

Top Ten Body Parts Injured Most Often in a Shark Attack

1 Calf/knee 34.6%
2 Arm 28.9%
3 Thigh 23.5 %
4 Foot 22.1%
5 Hand 12.8%
6 Abdomen/stomach 9.4%
7 Chest 8.7%
=8 Buttocks 7.4%
=8 Shoulder 7.4%
10 Back 6.7%

Source: International Shark Attack File, Florida Museum of Natural History

Top Ten Most Spectacular Comebacks

1 Escape to Victory, *Allies vs Germany 1944: Allies 4–0 down after 41 minutes but come back to draw 4-4.*

2 *Liverpool vs AC Milan,Champions League Final 2005: 3–0 down at half-time, Reds come back to draw 3–3 and win on penalties.*

3 *Manchester City vs Tottenham, FA Cup 2004: City were 3–0 down but come back to win 4–3 at White Hart Lane.*

4 *USSR vs Yugoslavia, 1952 Olympics: Yugoslavia lead 5–1 early in the second half. The Russians come back to draw 5–5.*

5 *Deportivo La Coruna vs AC Milan, Champions League quarter-final 2004: La Coruna were 4–1 down after the first leg but take Milan apart at the Riazor 4–0 to go through.*

6 *Partizan Belgrade vs QPR, Uefa Cup 2nd Round, 1984: QPR tear the Yugoslavs apart at Loftus Road, winning the 1st leg 6–2. Then lose the return leg 4–0 and go out on the away goal.*

7 *Portugal vs North Korea, World Cup quarter-final, 1966: Eusebio's lot find themselves 3–0 down to Korea before reverting to type and winning 5–3.*

8 *Bayern Munich vs Bayern Uerdingen, German Cup 1986: Munich are 5–1 down on aggregate with 33 minutes left but galvanize themselves somehow to come back and win 7–5.*

9 *West Germany vs England, World Cup quarter-final 1970: England, the World Champions are cruising and two up with 20 minutes left. Nauseatingly, the Germans fight back to win 3–2 and we've never recovered.*

10 *Tottenham vs Southampton, FA Cup 5th Round, 1995: Spurs are two down at half-time but hit back at the Dell with six second half goals, including a Ronny Rosenthal hat-trick.*

Top Ten Packets of Crisps Sold in the UK

Walkers is Britain's most popular snack brand. But which of their flavours sells best?

1. *Cheese and Onion crisps*
2. *Ready-salted crisps*
3. *Cheesy Quavers*
4. *Salt & Vinegar crisps*
5. *Prawn Cocktail crisps*
6. *Thai Sweet Chilli Sensations*
7. *Flamin' Hot Monster Munch*
8. *Pickled Onion Monster Munch*
9. *Cheesy Wotsits*
10. *Roast Chicken crisps*

Top Ten Brands Mentioned in Songs

1 Mercedes – 100 mentions
2 Nike – 63 mentions
3 Cadillac – 62 mentions
4 Bentley – 51 mentions
5 Rolls-Royce – 46 mentions
6 Hennessy Cognac – 44 mentions
7 Chevrolet – 40 mentions
8 Louis Vuitton – 35 mentions
9 Cristal champagne – 28 mentions
10 AK-47 assault rifles – 33 mentions

Source: lyrics US Top 200 singles during 2006

Top Ten Places Britons Like To Have Sex

1. Hotel room
2. Outside in the sunshine
3. Bath
4. Kitchen
5. Woods
6. Planes
7. Car
8. Weddings
9. Bed
10. The beach

Top Ten British pub names According to CAMRA

1. The Crown, 704 pubs
A recent number one, as more pubs called The Red Lion have closed than royalist Crowns. A popular pub name for 600 years (except for a gap during the Cromwell Commonwealth).
2. The Red Lion, 668 pubs
When King James VI of Scotland became James I of England too in 1603, he decreed that all public buildings should display the red lion of Scotland.
3. The Royal Oak, 541 pubs
The name comes from King Charles II's attempt to hide from the Roundheads by shinning up an oak in Shropshire, during the Civil War in 1651.
4. The Swan, 451 pubs
Many noble families had a swan in their coat of arms, so this is often a tribute to the local landowner. In the Midlands, it often refers to Shakespeare, the "Swan of Avon".
5. The White Hart, 431 pubs
This was 14th century King Richard II's nickname. History does not record whether he liked a pint.
6. The Railway, 420 pubs
Most of these pubs were opened next to the new railway stations, during the Victorian growth of the steam railway.
7. The Plough, 413 pubs
Despite pub signs often showing the constellation, this refers to agriculture. Farm hands going to The Plough after a hard day's work – that's like us going to The PC and Mobile for a pint.
8. The White Horse, 379 pubs
Popular in Kent, because it's the county symbol; in pubs near chalk horse figures; and pubs opened in the 18th and 19th centuries, during the reign of Hanoverian monarchs (white horse crest)
9. The Bell, 378 pubs
Usually used by pubs close to churches. Subtle hint to go and sing a hymn or two before getting ratted on a Sunday lunchtime.
10. The New Inn, 372 pubs
Usually the second pub in a village whose population had grown, ironically there are New Inns dating back to the 16th Century.

TOP TEN REJECTED BAND NAMES

1. Pectoralz – Coldplay
2. Bastard – Mötorhead
3. The Rain – Oasis
4. On A Friday – Radiohead
5. Faecal Matter – Nirvana
6. Seymour – Blur
7. The Strand – The Libertines
8. The Hype – U2
9. The Lotus Eaters – Keane
10. Dead Lesbian and the Fibrillating Scissor Sisters – Scissor Sisters

Top Ten Grossing Films of All Time

(adjusted for inflation)

1. Gone With the Wind, *$2,700m*
2. Snow White and the Seven Dwarfs, *$2,699m*
3. Titanic, *$2,245m*
4. Star Wars Episode IV: A New Hope, *$1,438m*
5. Jurassic Park, *$1,236m*
6. Bambi, *$1,191m*
7. The Lord of the Rings: The Return of the King, *$1,187m*
8. Harry Potter and the Philosopher's Stone, *$1,077m*
9. Star Wars: Episode I: The Phantom Menace, *$1,054m*
10. The Lion King, *$1,032m*

Top 10 Britain's Least Rock 'n' Roll Towns

With their most musical son or daughter. As voted by rockingvicar.com

1. *Milton Keynes – nobody. Fact.*
2. *Plymouth – ditto (but Dawn French studied there and once appeared on a Comic Relief single with Bananarama*
3. *Doncaster – John Parr (one-hit wonder with St Elmo's Fire)*
4. *Reading – Morning Runner (plus Ricky Gervais of Free Love Highway fame and a rock festival)*
5. *Dunstable – Faye Tozer out of Steps*
6. *Clacton – 80s crooning model Sade*
7. *Batley – Robert Palmer*
8. *Ipswich – Charlie out of Busted*
9. *Peterborough – Andy Bell out of Erasure*
10. *Eastbourne – Toploader*

Top Ten Most Expensive Cities To Live In

1. **Oslo, Norway**
2. **Tokyo, Japan**
3. **Reykjavik, Iceland**
4. **Osaka, Japan**
5. **Paris, France**
6. **Copenhagen, Denmark**
7. **London, England**
8. **Zurich, Switzerland**
9. **Geneva, Switzerland**
10. **Helsinki, Finland**

Top Ten Pound-for-pound fighters in the world, according to boxing bible Ring

1. Floyd Mayweather Jnr
2. Manny Pacquiano
3. Ronaldo "Winky" Wright
4. Marco Antonio Barrera
5. Jermain Taylor
6. Bernard Hopkins
7. Oscar De La Hoya
8. Joe Calzaghe
9. Antonio Margarito
10. Ricky Hatton

Top 10 Richest British Comedians

1. Tracey Ullman, £75 million

   Eighties comic has shares in *The Simpsons*, which started on her US show

2. Rowan Atkinson, £40 million

   No-translation-required idiot Mr Bean sells worldwide, plus shares in Tiger Aspect (makers of *The Vicar Of Dibley*)

3. Jasper Carrott, £35 million

   Brummie owns shares in *Who Wants To Be A Millionaire?*

4. John Cleese, £30 million

   The not-funny-since-the-therapy Python made his dosh from films and his training video empire

5. = Griff Rhys-Jones, £25 million

   The ruined building-botherer made money from selling Talkback production company (*Partridge*, *Buzzcocks*, *Ali G*)

5. = Mel Smith, £25 million

   The big-boned balding one from *Smith & Jones* also made his cash flogging Talkback to Thames

7. Steve Coogan, £11 million

   Much of his cash comes from *Partridge* DVDs and Baby Cow Productions (*Boosh*, *Nighty Night*)

8. Jennifer Saunders, £10 million

   From Ab Fab success and co-owns production company Mr & Mrs Monsoon with ex-Young Ones hubbie Ade Edmonson

9. Eddie Izzard, £9.5 million

   The funny tranny has stormed the USA with live tours and DVDs, plus roles in movies including the Ocean's series and Jerry Seinfeld's *Bee Movie*

10. Peter Kay, £8 million

    To the annoyance of some of his co-writers, Kay has raked in most of the moolah from *Phoenix Nights*, as well as his solo work and huge-selling memoirs

Top Ten World's Most Expensive Wines

(and what to say about them)

1. Domaine Romane Conti 1997 £775
Rich red Burgundy: berries, soy sauce, liquorice

2. Petrus Pomerol 1998 £725
JFK's favourite wine, a Merlot

3. Chateau Le Pin Pomerol 1999 £450
A Bordeaux with black cherry and mocha flavour

4. Chateau Latour Pauillac 1990 £380
Given a rare perfect score by booze bible Wine Spectator

5. Chateau Valandraud Saint-Emilion 1995 £335
Comes from a tiny French vinyard of only 35 acres

6. Chateau La Mondotte Saint-Emilion 1996 £300
Even smaller vinyard (11 acres) producing a fruity number

7. Chateau Mouton Rothschild Pauillac 1986 £290
British family vinyard, famous for labels by artists including Picasso and Warhol

8. Chateau Haut Brion Pessac-Lognan 1982 £265
Chateau that produced the first ever Bordeaux

9. Chateau Margaux 1995 £200
Almost black red wine from a 1,000 year-old vinyard

10. Chateau Lafite Rothschild Pauillac 1996 £150
The favourite drink of King Louis XV of France

TOP TEN 200MPH SUPERCARS

1. Bugatti Veyron 253mph
2. McLaren F1 240mph
3. Koenigsegg CC 8S 240mph
4. Pagani Zonda C12S 220mph
5. Ferrari Enzo 218mph
6. Jaguar XJ220 217mph
7. Bugatti EB110 209mph
8. Mercedes McLaren SLR 208mph
9. Maserati MC12 206mph
10. Porsche Carrera GT 205mph

TOP TEN AVERAGE LIFETIME SEXUAL PARTNERS WORLDWIDE

1. TURKEY 14.5
2. AUSTRALIA 13.5
3. ITALY 11.8
4. SWITZERLAND 11.1
5. USA 10.7
6. JAPAN 10.2
7. UK 9.8
8. AUSTRIA 9.7
9. FRANCE 8.1
10. SINGAPORE 7.2

ZOO ONE-LINERS

Comedy's most efficient gags – maximum laughs per word guaranteed

"The moth. Pretty much a Seventies butterfly."

NOEL FIELDING

"One armed butlers, eh? They can take it – but they can't dish it out."

TIM VINE

"We've got new neighbours. He's got this German shepherd that craps on the lawn. And he's got a dog."

JASPER CARROT

"You'll never guess who I bumped into at Specsavers yesterday – everybody."

JIMMY CARR

"Old people. You can't beat them, can you? Pity."

PETER KAY

"Somebody complimented me on my driving today. They left a little note on the windscreen, it said, 'Parking Fine.'"

TIM VINE

"I went to a general store. They wouldn't let me buy anything specific."

STEVEN WRIGHT

"Nobody thought Mel Gibson could play a Scot but look at him now: alcoholic and a racist."

FRANKIE BOYLE

"A friend of mine died of dyslexia. He choked on his own Vimto."

DAVE SPIKEY

"Cats have got nine lives. Which makes them ideal for experimentation."

JIMMY CARR

"I went to see a go-go dancer. But she'd gone."

HARRY HILL

"What's another word for Thesaurus?"

STEVEN WRIGHT

"I got thrown out of the scouts for eating a brownie."

ROSS NOBLE

"Everyone hates you. Surely you remember that from school?"

DAVID BADDIEL'S PUT-DOWN TO A HECKLER AT THE COMEDY STORE

"Yeah I have a girlfriend. I've been going out with her for...sex."

STEWART FRANCIS, US STAND-UP

"If it becomes illegal to wear the veil at work, bee-keepers will be furious."

MILTON JONES

"I was reading this book called The History of Glue. *I couldn't put it down."*

TIM VINE

"Apparently you can tell a lot about people from what they're like."

HARRY HILL

"I had a great business plan: I was going to build bungalows for dwarfs. There was only one tiny flaw…"

JUSTIN EDWARDS

"I love to freak out shop assistants. They ask what size I need, and I say, 'Extra medium.'"

STEVEN WRIGHT

"My love life is terrible. The last time I was inside a woman was when I visited the Statue of Liberty."

WOODY ALLEN

"If you have a pear-shaped body, you shouldn't wear pear-coloured clothes. Or act juicy."

DEMETRI MARTIN

"As I was getting into my car, this bloke says to me 'Can you give me a lift?'
I said 'Sure, you look great, the world's your oyster, go for it.'"

TIM VINE

"I'll tell you what I love doing more than anything: trying to pack myself in a small suitcase. I can hardly contain myself."

PETER KAY

"The trouble with heroin is it's very moreish."

HARRY HILL

"Today I met a subliminal advertising executive – but only very briefly."

STEVEN WRIGHT

"My parents are from Glasgow. I was never smacked as a child. Well, maybe one or two grams to get me to sleep at night."

SUSAN MURRAY

"There'd be less litter in Britain if blind people were given pointed sticks."

ADAM BLOOM

"Two guys came knocking at my door once and said: 'We want to talk to you about Jesus.' I said: 'Oh, no, what's he done now?'"

KEVIN MCALEER

"I don't take drugs anymore… than the average touring funk band"

BILL HICKS

"I never sleep with fish. I'm halibut."

TIM VINE

"I have a really nice stepladder. Sadly, I never knew my real ladder."

HARRY HILL

"When my Grandad got ill, my Grandma used to rub lard into his back. He went downhill pretty fast after that."

MILTON JONES

"So I met this gangster who pulls up the back of people's pants. It was Wedgie Kray."

PETER KAY

"I'm still making love at 71, which is handy for me because I live at number 63."

BERNIE CLIFTON

"Before I got into comedy, I was a plumber for 150 years – although that's just an estimate."

GORDON SOUTHERN

"My dad used to keep Eskimos and alligators. He bred escalators. We got a lot of funny stairs."

MAREK LARWOOD

"Why is it always Tudor houses we mock?"

HARRY HILL

"I was in a bookstore the other day, there was a third off all titles. I bought The Lion, The Witch."

JIMMY CARR

"Velcro. What a rip-off."

TIM VINE

"Disabled loos. Ironically, the only loos big enough to run around in."

ADAM BLOOM

"They say being a hostage is difficult. But I could do that with my hands tied behind my back."

PHIL NICHOL

SEX

"I like my body and I like sex. So yeah, I'm good in bed. I used to be a dancer so I am very flexible. I'm naturally bendy. If blokes want to explore that quality, then it's up to them."

PRESENTER FEARNE COTTON GETS OUR MINDS BOGGLING

"I fancy women big time. I check them out far more than I check out men. Maybe I'd like to sleep with a woman. But not Beyonce. I don't think she's dirty enough."

BILLIE PIPER'S PROBABLY RIGHT. BUT AN ENDURING IMAGE ANYHOW

"British men spend on average 22 minutes on foreplay. Of course, that's spread out between all of us over the course of a year."

Jimmy Carr, *8 Out Of 10 Cats*

"If a woman's performing oral sex on me, I have to admit I will have a little look down. Usually just to think, 'Ugh, how could you?'"

FRANK SKINNER

**"My grandad died aged 93 while he was shagging my gran.
I said, 'That must have been awful.'
She said, 'Not really, I were asleep.'"**

Dave Spikey

"I'm not averse to being tied up in silk scarves. I like a man to take charge. There's something very sexy about being submissive."

DESPERATE HOUSEWIVES' EVA LONGORIA. NOTE TO SELF: BUY SILK SCARVES JUST IN CASE

"My girlfriends surprised me on my 80th birthday in the grotto with 18 girls, but I don't think I had sex with all of them. Maybe 11."

***Playboy* tycoon Hugh Hefner. Hard-knock life huh?**

"I'd like my wife on top of me eating doughnuts."

JONATHAN ROSS REVEALS HIS INNER HOMER

"Beware trim and tidy."

Think your missus is cheating on you? Then heed blonde sexpot Jenny McCarthy's advice

"Shane was a bit porky. At times it was like a bus was trying to have sex with me."

PORN BABE KELLY COOKE ON BIG-BONED SPINNER WARNEY

"You know you've hit rock bottom when you're taping Eurotrash. *There's no such thing as an ironic wank, sadly."*

AL MURRAY

"I've got a problem with breast-feeding. Whenever my friends' wives gave birth I'd be round all the time. I'd be like, 'Oh look at little Darren. Isn't he lovely? He's hungry, you know.' 'No, he's just been fed.' 'No, look, he's fucking starving.' 'No, seriously, he's just...' 'Look, just get your tits out or I'll kill it!'

Frank Skinner

"I was at the hospital for a blood test and I was stopped dead in my tracks by a sign which said, 'Family Planning Advice. Use The Back Entrance.'"

Dave Spikey

Q. What did Cinderella do when she got to the ball?

A. She gagged.

From the B3ta Book Of Sick Jokes

"I was recently asked to judge Mr Gay UK. I said no problem at all: he's against nature and he's going to hell."

JIMMY CARR

"Henry was very powerful and noisy. It was a romantic expression of one man's feelings for a vacuum cleaner."

Russell Brand podcasts about sex with a Henry vacuum cleaner

"What do atheists scream when they come?"

BILL HICKS

"I was stood in the kitchen and my husband came in. I said, 'Let's have it off on the floor.'
He said, 'Why?'
I said, 'Because I need to time an egg.'"

LILY SAVAGE

"I can't find a woman anywhere who will touch me with a shitty stick.
Fair enough. It is a bit of an unusual request."

Andrew Lawrence

How do you get a fat girl into bed?
Piece of cake.

"My grandad said, 'The problem with you lot, you think you invented sex!'
'Okay, Grandad,' I said, 'have you ever fucked Nana up the arse, pulled out and come on her tits?'
Turns out he had. That's what killed her."
Jimmy Carr

"I listen well to women, I'm very considerate. And I encourage them to show their feelings. Because, apparently, that's the best way to let you fuck them."
Reginald D Hunter

A woman walks into a pharmacy and asks if they sell extra-large condoms.
"Yes madam," says the chemist. "Would you like to know how much they are?"
"No thanks," she says, "but do you mind if I stand here and wait to see if anyone buys one?"

What's blue and sticky?

SMURF JIZZ

"Sex is like bridge. If you don't have a good partner, you'd better have a good hand."

Woody Allen

"There's this campaign, 'If you're having sex tonight, make sure you get consent.' What sort of society is this if we have to remind people not to rape? 'I'm going out tonight, few pints, some rape.' 'You can't rape. It's illegal. Saw it on telly.' 'What? You mean you're not allowed to rape?'"

RICKY GERVAIS

"I was there in the delivery room, I saw what happened. Now anything my wife wants, gets done. She's like, 'Change the diaper,' and I'm like, 'Absolutely, sorry about your vagina.'"

ADAM SANDLER ON OWING HIS WIFE FOR THE PAIN OF CHILDBIRTH

"I've got a friend who's fallen in love with two school bags. He's bisatchel."

Tim Vine

"FOR CHRISTMAS, MY MATES CLUBBED TOGETHER AND BOUGHT ME A SWEATER. I'D HAVE PREFERRED A MOANER OR A SCREAMER."

TAM COWAN, *DAILY RECORD*

"The only thing I like about myself is my huge willy."

Robbie Williams: massive dick

"After serving only three days of her prison sentence, Paris Hilton has been let out of jail. When asked about it, Paris said, 'Usually I'm not a fan of premature release.'"

CONAN O'BRIEN

"Ladies aren't throwing themselves at me enough. For the record, if any women see me on the street and assume I've only got one thing on my mind, they're probably right."

STEPHEN MERCHANT LAMENTS HIS LACK OF FEMALE GROUPIES

"The prison was scared Paris would go on hunger strike so they took all the porridge and flavoured it with sperm. She gained four pounds. But at one point, she went 'Ahh nooo, this has got porridge in it?'"

Frankie Boyle, *8 Out Of 10 Cats*

"I'd kiss the mole on Amy Winehouse's face and every tattoo on her body. And I'd stick my tongue in the gap where her tooth is missing. I love her."

David Gest on what he'd do if he were invisible for the day

"I read in a magazine that 68% of British men masturbate on a regular basis. How do they know? Anyone I ask never does it. Did it show up on the Richter scale?"

BILLY CONNOLLY

"A bloke goes to the doctor with bad headaches. The doctor says, 'Can I ask you a personal question? Do you masturbate?' He says, 'Sometimes.' Doctor goes, 'Magic, ain't it.'

Peter Kay

"I recently filled in a questionnaire that asked me who I'd like to sleep with, anyone living or dead? I put 'anyone living'."

Jimmy Carr

What do you call a lesbian with big fingers?

Hung

"Borat was fine. There's nothing sexier than a big handlebar moustache. Call me crazy."

Sacha Baron Cohen's fiancée Isla Fisher. Crazy.

My wife is a sex object – every time I ask for sex, she objects.

Why do women like orgasms?
So they can moan even when they're enjoying themselves.

What's the definition of trust?
Two cannibals giving each other a blowjob.

"Now we have gay bishops, official. I wonder if this will filter down into the game of chess? Bishops make all the same moves, but can only be taken from behind."
Jason Wood

What do you say to a virgin when she sneezes? Goes-in-tight!

"You know that look women get when they want sex? Me neither."

PETER KAY

What do you do if your girlfriend starts smoking?
Slow down and use some lubricant.

"If you're in a relationship and sex has got boring, try bondage. Get your lover, blindfold them, get some rope and chains, tie them to the bed or radiator, then go out and fuck someone else."

STEWART LEE

"I had hassle getting out tonight – I had to organise a baby sitter. I don't have children, I just find they're a lot cheaper than escorts."

JIMMY CARR

"I replaced the headlights in my car with strobe lights, so it looks like I'm the only one moving."

Steven Wright

"I know why they like me – I look good in or out of my top and I have a huge widger."

GORDON RAMSAY ON HIS GAY FANS

"Are there any women here who don't like giving blowjobs? I can't understand that. I had a woman at my last show go, 'Yeah, well have you ever tried it?' I said, 'Yeah. Almost broke my back.'" **Bill Hicks**

A man visits the doctor's because he has a severe stuttering problem. After a thorough examination, the doctor consults with the patient.
Doctor: "It appears that the reason for your stuttering is that your penis is about six inches too long and it is thus pulling on your vocal cords, and thereby causing you this annoying problem of stuttering."
"Ddddd octttor. Whhaaat cccan I dddo?"
The doctor scratches his forehead, thinks for a minute and states that there is a procedure where we can free up the strain on the vocal cords by removing the six inches from the penis and freeing him from this horrible problem. The patient stuttering badly states that this problem has caused him so much embarrassment as well as loss of employment that anything would be worth it. The doctor plans for the procedure. The operation is a success and six months later the patient comes in for his check up.
The patient says to the: "Doctor, the operation was a success. I have not stuttered since the operation. I have a great job and my self esteem is fantastic. However, there is one problem, my wife says that she sort of misses the great sex we used to have before the extra six inches were removed. So I was wondering if it is possible to reattach those six inches."
The doctor scratches his forehead, thinks for a minute and says: "I dddoonnnbt ttthhhhinkkkk thatttt wooould bbbbee posssssibbble!"

"My sons love my stripper pole. They use it more than me."
Pamela Anderson must be very proud of Brandon, nine, and Dylan, eight

Gongs Given at the 2007 AVN Porn Awards

1. *Best Anal-Themed Release:* Weapons of Ass Destruction 4 *(Jules Jordan Video)*
2. *Best Interracial Series:* My Hot Wife Is Fucking Blackzilla *(Hush Hush Entertainment/Digital Sin)*
3. *Best Transsexual Series:* Transsexual Prostitutes *(Devil's Film)*
4. *Best Foreign Feature :* Porn Wars: Episode 1 *(Private U.S.A. / Pure Play Media)*
5. *Best Specialty Release:* Fem-Dom Strap-On - Strap Attack 4 *(Joey Silvera/Evil Angel)*
6. *Best Specialty Release:* Squirting – Flower's Squirt Shower 3 *(Elegant Angel Productions)*
7. *Best Amateur Release:* Bang Bus 9 *(Bang Productions)*
8. *Best Anal-Themed Series:* Big Wet Asses *(Elegant Angel Productions)*
9. *Best Hard-Edged All-Sex Release:* Slave Dolls 2 *(Elegant Angel)*
10. *Best Group Sex Scene – Video:* Fashionistas Safado: The Challenge *(Evil Angel Productions), Belladonna, Melissa Lauren, Jenna Haze, Gianna, Sandra Romain, Adrianna Nicole, Flower Tucci, Sasha Grey, Nicole Sheridan, Marie Luv, Caroline Pierce, Lea Baren, Jewell Marceau, Jean Val Jean, Christian XXX, Voodoo, Chris Charming, Erik Everhard, Mr. Pete, Rocco Siffredi*

"Watching sex on telly with Mum and Dad – that's embarrassing. I didn't even know they had a camcorder."

Jimmy Carr

"Sure, I shave down there. I do it myself or I have my young lady help me, because I don't want to get no nicks."

SEAN 'DIDDY' COMBS ON HIS "DOWNSTAIRS"

"SEX EDUCATION AT MY SCHOOL WAS A MUTTERED WARNING ABOUT THE JANITOR." Frankie Boyle

"When a guy comes, he comes 200 million sperm. I've wiped entire civilisations off my chest with a grey gym sock."

Bill Hicks

"I GET PLANE-ONS, CAB-ONS, LIMO-ONS... MY DICK IS HARD ALL THE TIME. I DON'T THINK IT'S NORMAL."

TOMMY LEE ON HIS NON-STOP ERECTION

"At what stage do you get embarrassed about 'enlarge your penis' emails? I'm not the only one getting them, am I? It's just currently I'm getting about 10 a day. Eight of them are from my girlfriend. It's the two from my mum that really hurt." Jimmy Carr

"Sex and sleep are my two favourite things. If I could do both at the same time, I'd be a happy man. I always envy my girlfriend that trick." Ed Byrne

ZOO PUB TRIVIA

The leopard seal, native to the Antarctic, can consume an entire adélle penguin in four minutes, starting by skinning it alive on the water.

The sugar glider – a type of flying squirrel – can glide up to 148.5ft (45 metres).

Zebras are white with black stripes, not vice versa.

A radar has logged a peregrine falcon making a 1,000ft (305 metre) dive travelling at... 114mph. Which is still short of it's top speed: 124mph.

Of all known forms of animal ever to inhabit the Earth, only about 10 per cent still exist today.

Pandas love porn. A baby boom was sparked by Chinese scientists who showed a handful of the lazy, sex-shy bears a DVD of other pandas mating. The result? Almost a 250 per cent increase in births.

FIVE NEED-TO-KNOW NUGGETS ABOUT ANIMALS THAT MIGHT TAKE OVER THE WORLD

1. *Nine-year-old sea lion Jonao can paint letters. In Chinese. Here he is, brush in mouth and daubing "wild boar" at Hakkeijima Sea Paradise in suburban Tokyo. Today "wild boar", tomorrow… "attack the humans"?*
2. *Since 1935, cane toads introduced to Australia have multiplied at such a rate that now (population 200 million and destroying* everything *in their path), the Australian military has been called in to halt their advance on Darwin.*
3. *Animals can TALK. In English! A captive African grey parrot discovered in 2004 called N'kisi has an astonishing 950 word vocabulary. He uses words in context, with past, present and future tense, and even has a sense of humour.*
4. *Other creatures aren't far behind. South America's giant river otters have nine distinct vocalisations, which vary from screams of excitement to coos of recognition.*
5. *Earthquakes will decimate our cities and us, but not snakes. The spineless serpents can enjoy our planet once we're gone – they detect tremors up to 75 miles away, five days before it kicks off. At which point, they leave their nests en masse.*

ALL PORCUPINES FLOAT IN WATER.

As of December 2006, China has fluorescent pigs. The DNA of a bioluminescent jellyfish was implanted in to a sow and three piglets were born 114 days later with mouths, trotters and hooves that glow green under UV light.

In 1945 a chicken survived for two years after having its head cut off. The axe missed the jugular vein and left enough of the brain stem for the poultry to survive.

A walrus' tusks can grow up to one metre in length.

Each year, insects eat one third of the Earth's entire food crop.

Roosters can't crow unless they fully extend their neck.

There are only two known animals with blue tongues: the black bear and the chow dog.

In the last 4000 years, no new animals have been domesticated.

In 2007, a New York man blinded in his right eye 64 years ago by WWII shrapnel, regained his sight after being head butted by a pedigree racehorse.

The Yanomami Indians of South America call the jaguar "Eater of Souls", due to their belief that it consumes the spirits of the dead.

The Arctic fox can withstand temperatures as low as -50 degrees Celsius.

The chiffchaff – a small bird that visits the UK in the summer – is so-called as its two-note song sounds like 'chiff chaff'.

WILDLIFE IN NUMBERS

- 20 – lbs lost by Pongo the dalmatian to win the accolade of Britain's Top Pet Slimmer 2006.
- 47 – average number of teeth in a mosquito's mouth.
- 80 – live rats escaped on a Saudi Airlines flight at 25,000ft late 2006.
- 5 million – average number of eggs laid in one go by the mola mola, or ocean sunfish.
- 7 – length in feet of the carpet pythons found in an Australian school teacher's U-bend after she complained of a blockage.
- 60 – maximum flight speed (in mph) of the dragonfly.
- 0.0313 – speed in (mph) of the fastest-moving the common garden snail – the fastest snail.
- 14 – million camels on planet Earth.
- 250 – miles a king penguin will travel in search of food for its chick.
- 200,000 – glasses of milk a cow will fill during her lifetime.
- 26 – cycles per second a cat purrs at, frequency fans. Which is the same cycle rate as an idling diesel engine.
- 1– dogs in the US estimated to be named as the primary beneficiary in their owner's will (in millions).

GOAT'S EYES HAVE RECTANGULAR PUPILS

Emus cannot walk backwards.

The bones of a pigeon weigh less than its feathers.

Goats do not eat tin cans. They simply nibble at them for the tasty glue found beneath the labels.

The honey possum has the largest testes to body size of any mammal. Its balls weigh 4.2 per cent of its body weight.

The northern right whale is named thus only because hunters originally thought it the "right whale" to kill.

Snow leopards can bring down prey three times their own size.

The world's heaviest insect is the wetapunga (aka demon grasshopper). The largest ever on record weighed 71g.

Ratty from Wind In The Willows was actually a water vole, not a rat. The creatures are commonly mistaken for one another.

Tiger sharks are nicknamed "the dustbin of the sea" as they not only eat anything in their path including other sharks, but also eat rubbish itself.

The world's smallest primate is the pygmy mouse lemur.

They measure just 6.1cm.

Jungle cats – native to Egypt, the Middle East, southern Asia and western China – are the only cats that bark.

Unlike domestic turkeys fattened up for festive slaughter, wild turkeys can fly short distances at speeds up to 55mph.

The common goldfish is the only animal that can see both infra-red and ultra-violet light.

Neither rats, rabbits nor horses can vomit.

Cats in Halifax, Nova Scotia, have a very high probability of having six toes.

A pregnant goldfish is called a twit.

Twelve or more cows are known as a flink.

The poisonous copperhead snake smells like freshly cut cucumbers.

The largest animal ever seen alive was a 113.5 foot, 170-ton female blue whale.

JUKEBOX FAVOURITES AT THE GOOD MIXER

1. *America* Razorlight
2. *Rehab* Amy Winhouse
3. *Love Train* Wolfmother
4. *Run* Snow Patrol
5. *Time For Heroes* The Libertines
6. *The Harder They Come* Jimmy Cliff
7. *White Riot* The Clash
8. *The View From Here* Arctic Monkeys
9. *Paint It Black* Rolling Stones
10. *Feeling Good* Muse

Thanks to the legendary indie drinking hole in London's scuzzy Camden – especially owner Sarah Hurley and barman Chris Langridge.

CARS IN NUMBERS

The McLaren F1's engine bay is lined with 24-carat gold foil.

Fernando Alonso drove the same Renault F1 car in every Grand Prix in 2006.

The Jaguar XJ220 never lived up to its name because it never did 220 mph. Martin Brundle managed to coax 217.1 mph out of it.

The original Golf GTI weighed a mere 810kg. The Mk V model GTI was 526kg heavier.

The paddle-shift transmission in a Ferrari 599 GTB can change gears in 100 milliseconds, almost as fast as an F1 car.

The first Porsche 911 Turbo launched in 1974 has 256bhp and topped out at 155 mph. The current Turbo has 480 bhp and a 195mph top speed.

- The 1965 Renault 16 was the world's first five-door hatchback.
- A top-fuel dragster will hit 170 mph in 7.9 seconds.
- The Volkswagen Beetle was in continuous production for 58 years – the longest run of any car ever.
- The Lexus Ls is fitted with a 19 speaker Mark Levinson stereo hooked up to a hard drive capable of holding up to 4,000 songs.
- The Fiat 500 of 1957 was powered by an air-cooled two-cylinder engine that produced just 13bhp for a 55 mph top speed.
- In 1987 a Bugatti Royale Kelner Coupe sold at auction for £4,913,000, the most expensive car to ever go under the hammer.
- Between 1908 and 1927, 15million Model T Fords were produced.
- At 3.2seconds the Caterham R500 is quicker to 60 mph than a McLaren F1 and Ferrari Enzo.
- Stuffed with expensive impact monitoring equipment, the average crash test dummy costs £100,000.
- Xenon headlamp bulbs are about the size of a match head and need around 25,000 volts to produce any light.
- The Knowledge test every London black cab driver must pass involves knowing every street within a six-mile radius of Charing Cross.
- Audi's Quattro all-wheel-drive system was designed by VW boss Ferdinand Piech, the same man who instigated the Bugatti Veyron and purchased Bentley, Lamborghini and Cosworth.
- The Bugatti Type 35 of 1924 was the most successful racing car of all time, racking up 1,000 wins in five years.
- In Japan, Toyota sells cars called the Windom, Belta, Kluger, Funcargo and Ractis.
- On full afterburn, the Thrust SSC's twin Spey 205 jet engines each produce 25,000lb of thrust, around 55,000bhp.
- Honda has never had a single warranty claim on any of its V-TEC engines.
- TVR, which went into administration this month, was named after its founder TreVoR Wilkinson.
- When Vauxhall launched the 176 mph Lotus Carlton, *The Daily Mail* was so incensed by its top speed that it mounted a public campaign to ban it.
- The Ferrari FXX has 40% more downforce than a standard Enzo.
- The 350 mph JCB Dieselmax world speed record holder is powered by two engines, each producing 750 bhp.
- The Quandt family, which owns just under half of BMW is valued at £10 billion.
- The Heuer Monaco, the watch immortalised by Steve McQueen in *Le Mans* was the first automatic chronograph in the world.

Five need-to-know nuggets about...

THE BUGATTI VEYRON

1. *With a 0–62 mph time of 2.5 seconds, the Veyron is quicker off the mark than a F18 Hornet jet fighter accelerating for take-off on full afterburners.*
2. *The Bugatti's W16 engine is actually two twin-turbo 4.0-litre V8 engines mounted alongside each other on a common crankcase.*
3. *To achieve full speed, the driver has to switch on a Speed Key, which retracts the rear spoiler to reduce drag and boost speed.*
4. *The mid-mounted engine has no cover – the polished aluminium alloy air intakes and cam covers are open to the elements to help keep the engine cool.*
5. *At full throttle in seventh gear the Veyron returns 2.8 mpg, which means it runs its 22-gallon fuel tank dry in just 20 minutes.*

- Honda turned to F1 world champion Ayrton Senna to help design its NSX supercar.
- The Porsche GT3 RS has a plastic rear windscreen to save weight.
- In 1996, 1997 and 1998 Maserati did not sell one car in the UK.
- Audi's mid-engined R8 supercar features an incredible 210 external LED lights used in the head and tail lamps.
- The Corvette Z06 uses balsa wood in the construction of its lightweight chassis.
- After Goldfinger was launched, in which Bond drove an Aston Martin DB5, Aston's sales rocketed by 60%.
- BP's Ultimate 102 petrol costs £10.78 a gallon, two and a half times the cost of regular unleaded.
- The Ferrari F40 was the first supercar to break the 200 mph barrier with a 201 mph top speed, 3 mph more than its deadliest rival the Porsche 959.

- The first supercar was the 350bhp V12 Lamborghini Miura, which made its debut in 1966. CAR magazine coined the term 'supercar' to describe it.
- During a pedestrian impact, small explosive charges in the Jaguar XK's bonnet fire to pop up the bonnet and protect the pedestrian's head from the engine.
- The Bugatti EB110's tiny 2.5-litre V12 engine used four turbochargers to produce a massive 553bhp.
- Knight Rider's KITT car took its name from the acronym of Knight Industries Two Thousand.

Motoring in numbers!

- 13.5million – the number of driver who had points put on their licence in 2006.
- 86,400 – the cost in pounds of the M6 Convertible, BMW's most expensive car.
- 1,369 – the number of F1 points Michael Schumacher scored in his career, the highest to date.
- 137 – the number of times a second each rotor in the Mazda RX-8's engine turns at peak power.
- 140 – the number of horsepower VW manages to squeeze out of its tiny 1.4-litre supercharged and turbocharged Golf engine.
- 6.75 – the size in litres of the Rolls-Royce Phantom Drophead's V12 engine.
- 60 – the number of seconds it takes Toyota's Valenciennes factory in France to produce one Yaris.
- 2,855 – the weight in kilogrammes of the Maybach 62.
- 8 – the number of forward gears in the Lexus LS460's gearbox.
- 16 – the number of model types in the Mercedes range, more than any other carmaker in the UK.
- 18.9 – the average number of miles the Range Rover Vogue can travel on one gallon of petrol.
- 20 – the percentage of people killed in car crashes with illegal drugs in their blood stream.
- 1,012 – the number of horsepower the Bristol Fighter S's biturbo 8.0-litre V10 produces.
- 350.8 – the speed in miles per hour that Chris Carr achieved on his Streamliner motorbike to set a new land speed motorbike record late 2006.
- 170 – the speed in miles per hour of the Lamborghini Miura, the world's first supercar.

Top Drinking & Pub Games

1. ***Bullshit poker***
   Each player has a note in his hand (originally a dollar bill) and takes in turns to make bids of the highest "hand" in the combined notes – one might bid four 7s, the next three 8s, another four 8s, and the last guy a pair of 10s (represented by 0s, 1s, aces, are high). Eventually someone challenges this with a "Bullshit!" If it's actually true, you each pay the bidder, if it's not, he pays each of you.
2. ***Spoof***
   You all have three coins in one hand. Transfer between none and three to your right hand and hold it out, closed. Take it in turns to guess how many total coins there are in all fists. Get it right and you drop out. Last man in buys the next round.
3. ***Big Lebowski***
   You have to match the Dude drink for drink (White Russians – vodka, Kahlua, milk). Some naughty folk also match him toke for toke.
4. ***The Beer Hunter***
   Russian roulette with a four-pack instead of a pistol. One can gets shaken up, then everyone takes a can at random and opens it while pointing at your head.
5. ***Drink while you think***
   The first player names a celebrity, say Ricky Gervais, then the next has to name one whose first name starts with the same letter as the surname, so George Michael. If the next player uses a one-named celeb, say Madonna, it carries on with M as the first initial; if it's a double letter, say Mandy Moore, it bounces it back the way it came. You drink while it's your turn till you say a name. In the extreme version, other players can be shouting names you can't have.
6. ***Roxanne***
   Divide your group into two teams and put 'Roxanne' by The Police on the jukebox/stereo. When Sting sings "Roxanne", one team drinks; when the he sings "Put on the red light", the other team drinks. Simple.
7. ***Yard of ale***
   Try to beat the last world records listed (5.5 seconds for a three-pint yard set by a drinker at Corby Town FC, 5 seconds for the 2.5pint by RAF Upper Heyford, both from 1976) before Guinness succumbed to "responsible drinking" pressure in the 90s.
8. ***Star Wars***
   Drink every time the Force is mentioned. In the original films, drink every time some one says "Luke". In Episodes I to III, swap that for Anakin.
9. ***Headmaster***
   As an addition to any other drinking game, one player is the "headmaster". When he puts his head on the table, the last person to get their head down has to skull. Usually ends up with a couple headbutting the table.

So far, 209 planets outside our galaxy have been discovered. Most are bigger than Jupiter, the biggest planet in our Solar System.

Man has not visited any other planet yet – only the Moon.

The Moon was created when the early Earth banged into another early version of a planet. A chunk of planet was spat out and got caught in the Earth's gravitational pull.

The Moon is 384,399 km away from Earth, meaning it takes light reflected off the Moon's surface 1.3 seconds to reach us.

The craters on the moon are a result of asteroids and comets smashing into it over the last few billion years. The lack of any atmosphere or weather means they've all been preserved. The largest crater is 13km deep and 2,240km across – about 50 times the size of the UK.

The Outer Space Treaty – signed by all major countries in 1967 – means no-one is allowed to claim any part of the moon's surface. It also means weapons or any form of military installation are forbidden.

Earth only has one moon. Jupiter has 63 and Saturn has 56.

Despite only being roughly eleven times bigger in size, Jupiter weighs 317 times as much as Earth.

Pluto was considered the most distant of the nine planets in the Solar System until 2006, when an official definition of a planet was drawn up by the International Astronomical Union. It's now considered to be a "dwarf planet".

The further away a planet is from the Sun, the longer its year. A year on Neptune, 30 times further from the Sun than us, the most distant planet, is the equivalent to 164 years on Earth. A day on Venus is the equivalent to 243 Earh days.

The Sun accounts for 99.86% of the Solar System's total mass. Jupiter and Saturn account for more than 90% of the remaining mass.

The Sun is roughly halfway through its life. It was only 75 per cent as bright early in its history and it's getting brighter as it gets older. In about five billion years, it will blow up.

Venus is the planet closest to Earth, but being a bit closer to the Sun, it gets hotter: about 400 degrees C.

The temperature on the surface of the Sun is thought to be about 5,727 degrees C.

SIZE OF A PLANET!

The solar systems proportions in terms we can all understand...

The Sun = Big Ben's clock face
Jupiter = Standard car wheel
Saturn = Large Domino's Pizza
Uranus = Basketball
Neptune = Football
Earth = Tennis ball
Venus = Orange
Mars = Golf ball
Mercury = Polo mint
The Moon = 5p piece

Great Hangover Cures In Numbers

10 – hours of sleep.
9 – pints of water.
8 – hours of watching porn.
7 – cans of Coke.
6 – bags of Cheesy Doritos.
5 – Bloody Mary's.
4 – heart attacks on a roll (bacon, egg and extra grease).
3 – wanks.
2 – blowjobs.
1 – big dump.

Every episode of *Seinfeld* contains a small homage to Superman – whether it's a mention of him, a background pic or even Jerry wearing red and blue.

Little Britain sketches filmed on the same day in the same swimming pool filled two of the top five places in Channel 4's *50 Greatest Comedy Sketches Of All Time* poll – Lou and Andy's diving board gag and Vicky Pollard pissing in the water.

Matt Lucas's cousin, Alexa Tilley, was a contestant on* The Apprentice. *Alan Sugar told her, "You're fired".

The live stage show of *Bottom* was so violent that both Ade Edmonson and Rik Mayall were hospitalised at various times.

The *Father Ted* theme tune was written and performed by The Divine Comedy and a version of it appears on their *Casanova* album, along with a track called "Woman Of The World", his first stab at the theme tune, which was rejected.

Jack Dee has appeared on Jonathan Ross's chat show six times – the most sofa spots by any celebrity.

The poster behind Larry's secretary's desk in *Curb Your Enthusiasm* changes every episode.

Jennifer Saunders got her Absolutely Fabulous *character's name, Edina Monsoon, from her husband Ade Edmonson's university nickname, Eddie Monsoon.*

DAVE GORMAN PREPARES FOR LIVE SHOWS IN HIS DRESSING ROOM BY BALANCING PEBBLES ON TOP OF EACH OTHER

Jerry Springer – The Opera creator Stewart Lee compulsively collects all the miniature toiletries in every hotel he stays in.

Ricky Gervais's 80s New Romantic band Seona Dancing only had one top 10 hit – in the Philippines.

Jimmy Carr has a pink orchid named after him.

There are two statues of comedians in Douglas on the Isle of Wight – one of Norman Wisdom and one of George Formby. There are none in Norwich, after the City Council refused to give planning permission for a 60-foot statue of Alan Partridge.

Two thieves were jailed after stealing £200,000 from Ricky Gervais's bank account, using a picture from one of his DVDs pasted into a dead man's passport as ID.

In 2005 Sacha Baron Cohen returned to the Israeli kibbutz where he spent part of his gap year and coached the Frisbee team to a tournament victory.

ANT AND DEC HAVE TAKEN OUT INSURANCE SO EACH GETS A £2 MILLION PAYOUT IF THE OTHER ONE DIES UNEXPECTEDLY.

Thick Of It *and* Day Today *creator Armando Iannucci was offered the Radio 1 breakfast show in the 90s – after he refused, it went to Steve Wright instead*

***Father Ted* co-creator Graham Linehan based the Father Jack Hackett character on one of the priests at his secondary school.**

In a deleted scene on the Pirates of the Caribbean *DVD,* Fast Show *obsessive Johnny Depp uses the "I'll get me coat" catchphrase.*

Before he was famous, Jerry Seinfeld made money selling fake jewellery and was involved in a telemarketing scam.

***PEEP SHOW'S* MITCHELL AND WEBB WROTE SKETCHES FOR ARMSTRONG & MILLER, *DEAD RINGERS* AND *BIG TRAIN*.**

Pop piss-taker Weird Al Jankovic failed to get clearance to release a James Blunt parody single called "You're Pitiful".

Mirth In Numbers

2 – fans who turned up to a Ben Elton book signing in Carlisle in January 2006.

16 – times black comedian Damon Wayons dropped the n-bomb at LA's Laugh Factory the week after Michael 'Kramer' Richards' racist rant. It earned Wayans a fine and a suspension from the venue, whose owners had banned the word, but he said, "I'll be damned if the white man uses that word last."

95 – per cent of University of Maryland test subjects whose blood flow was increased by watching comedy, equivalent to mild aerobic exercise.

201 – Swear words used in a single TV show (one every nine seconds), a world record set by Paul Kay in *Strutter*, beating *South Park*'s previous best, 162.

Stephen Fry was not originally intended to be the host of *QI* – the producers wanted Michael Palin.

Zeppo Marx invented the bomb clasps ('Marman clamps') on the bomber *Enola Gay*, which released the A-bomb over Hiroshima.

The only Blackadder series where Edmund Blackadder does not die at the end is the third, when he plays the Prince Regent's butler.

When Fawlty Towers is broadcast in Spain, waiter Manuel's nationality is changed to Italian.

Prince Philip protested that Catherine Tate had gone too far during the Royal Variety Show *when her "bovvered" character Lauren commented that "the old fella next to the Queen" appeared to be asleep.*

Men Behaving Badly *star Martin Clunes collects and restores VW camper vans.*

Jimmy Carr got 4 A grades at A-level.

Writer John Sullivan initially gave *Only Fools And Horses* the working title *Readies* but eventually decided a longer name would grab viewers' attention.

Fast Show star Simon Day claimed he based his Competitive Dad character on a man he once saw at a swimming pool, who challenged his two young children to a race and then swam away at top speed, leaving them struggling at the other end.

THE VICAR OF DIBLEY IS FILMED IN TURVILLE IN BUCKINGHAMSHIRE – ALSO THE LOCATION OF MIDSOMER MURDERS.

The shop used in the exterior shots in *Open All Hours* is actually a hairdressers.

The four most common references in Eddie Izzard's stand-up routines – according to avid fans – are jam, banjos, bananas and the Bible.

Comedy In Numbers

2 – heart attacks suffered by Richard Pryor, in a life also featuring six divorces, eight children, a prostitute mother and near-fatal burns from freebasing.

7.5 – Years longer than the actual Korean War (three years) that M*A*S*H *ran on TV.*

$38 million – dollars made by the Original Kings of Comedy tour, featuring Ocean's Eleven *star Bernie Mac and three other leading black comedians, the most successful comedy tour ever.*

150 – one-liners (sample: "I put instant coffee in a microwave – I nearly went back in time") told by stone-faced Steven Wright in his 60-minute US TV special – 2.5 laughs a minute.

230 – F-words used by Eddie Murphy in Delirious *stage show*

£300 million – raised by Comic Relief since it started in 1985.

700 – lengths of an Olympic swimming pool equivalent to the 22-mile cross-Channel swim completed by David Walliams.

5 – foreign versions of The Office *– the US version with Steve Carell, the French* Le Bureau *(Brent is called David Gervais), French-Canadian* La Job*, plus German and Brazilian comedies strongly modelled on it.*

7 – British Comedy Awards won by David Walliams and Matt Lucas, more than anyone else. Ant & Dec are second with 6.

Peter Kay is a qualified stand-up comedian… it was a module on his Media Performance Studies BTec course.

MPs recently voted *Yes Minister* the best political comedy, ahead of *Spitting Image* and *Bremner, Bird and Fortune*, but *The Thick Of It* didn't make the top 10.

Peep Show *creator Sam Bain's granny was one of the old ladies who were permanent residents at Fawlty Towers.*

Russell Brand is a vicar – at least he has been ordained as a minister over the internet so he could officiate at a friend's wedding.

In 1997 The Chris Rock Show *ran a joke about an OJ Simpson instructional video called "I didn't murder my wife but if I had, this is how I'd have done it" – nine years before OJ wrote a book about exactly that.*

Chris Morris's strict Jesuit religious school, Stoneyhurst, was the subject of a police investigation into child abuse – pupils were allegedly beaten with a whale bone.

A script assistant tried to sue the producers of *Friends* for sexual harrassment because of the rude jokes she had to type out during script meetings – she lost.

Torchwood's Captain Jack, John Barrowman was down to the last three to play Will in *Will & Grace* but was rejected for not being gay enough. The part went to the straight Eric McCormack.

ARDAL O'HANLON'S DAD IS THE SPEAKER OF THE DAÍL, THE IRISH HOUSE OF COMMONS.

Michael Palin once appeared in a cameo as a nervous British surfer in Home And Away.

The face of Dale Gribble, the hapless conspiracy theorist neighbour in *King Of The Hill,* is based on T-1000 actor Robert Patrick.

Dylan Moran, stand-up and red wine-swilling Bernard from *Black Books*, got married on the day of Princess Diana's funeral, not far from Westminster Abbey.

In a *Spaced* spoof of a scene from *The Sixth Sense,* the dead cyclist who appears at Simon Pegg's window is played by Olivia Williams – who plays Bruce Willis's wife in *The Sixth Sense.*

The Futurama *theme tune samples the drums from James Brown's* Funky Drummer.

Royston Vasey, the village in *The League Of Gentlemen*, is the real name of Roy 'Chubby' Brown who plays its mayor.

The music in South Park *whenever Satan's son Damien appears sounds like the scary 'Ave Satani' from* The Omen *but in fact they are chanting 'Rectus Dominus [ass master]... Cheesy Poofs'*

Five Need-to-know Nuggets about *The Simpsons*

1. *Names of characters have been known to change – Mafia boss Fat Tony's surname has been Balducci, D'Amico and Williams. Krusty's real name has been both Herschel Schmoikel Krustofski and Herschel Pinkus Yerucham Krustofski.*
2. *Only Homer, Bart and Lisa have dialogue in every episode (Marge appears but does not speak in "Krusty Gets Kancelled").*
3. *Creator Matt Groening named "Bart The Daredevil" (where Bart attempts to jump Springfield Gorge on his skateboard) as his "best episode ever".*
4. *The family's middle names are JoJo (Bart), Marie (Lisa) and simply J (Homer). Marge and Maggie have none.*
5. *The characters were originally drawn with yellow skin to attract the attention of channel-hoppers.*

Bill Gates' personal fortune is five times the Gross Domestic Product of Iceland. He's given away over $29 billion to charities since 2000.

An average of $2 million per 30 seconds was paid for advertisers for slots during the last-ever episode of *Friends*. The show was seen by 51.1 million Americans.

IT COSTS 5.7 CENTS PER NOTE TO PRODUCE AMERICAN PAPER CURRENCY.

During the Civil War period, the Bureau of Engraving and Printing was called upon to print paper notes in denominations of 3 cents, 5 cents, 10 cents, 25 cents, and 50 cents. People hoarded coins because of their intrinsic value which created a drastic shortage of circulating coins.

Gary Glitter's autobiography reveals him so caught up in image that he felt it was his 'duty to his fans' to drink vintage champagne at over £2,000 a bottle at all times.

The most expensive hotel in the world is the Emirates Palace in Abu Dhabi. It costs over £8,000 a night to stay there.

The world's highest denomination note is the Hungarian 100 million B-Pengo, issued in 1946. That's 100,000,000,000,000,000,000 pengo.

On May 2, 1990, John Goddard was mugged at knife-point during his daily courier round from Sheppard's money brokers in London. His briefcase contained bearer bonds worth a total of £292 million.

The world's most expensive phone number was auctioned for charity in Qatar in 2006. The number 666 6666 sold for £1.5m.

U2 WERE THE WORLD'S TOP-EARNING MUSIC ACT IN 2005 WITH AN INCOME OF £146,371,252.

The term 'buck' originated from the Old West when buckskin was a common medium of barter exchange with Indians.

MTV was offered to CNN media mogul Ted Turner before it launched in 1981 for half a million dollars. Turner refused thinking it was 'A complete joke and a failure waiting to happen'.

The Japanese Government issued bank notes, known as Japanese Invasion Money (JIMs) during WWII in its five occupied territories.

The most expensive residence in the world is Updown Court in Windlesham, Surrey. Currently valued at £70 million, it has 103 rooms including squash court, bowling alley, heated marble driveway, five swimming pools, 24-carat gold leafing on the study's mosaic floor and an underground garage with room for eight limousines.

In response to the 2004 Asian tsunami, governments worldwide pledged enormous sums of aid but most ended up paying much less. Germany came out worst, paying only 26.2 per cent of the $313 million they promised.

Rolling Stones guitarist Keith Richards' weekly bills between in 1971 were: £1,000 on food, £1,000 alcohol, £2,500 drugs and £2,500 rent on his Cote d'Azur villa. Fortunately this total was less than a third of his weekly income.

On average across Europe, men still earn 15% more than women. The disparity is worst in Germany, where there is a 23% gap.

There were more £20 notes issued in 2006 (341 million) than any other note.

With a wealth of £14.9 billion, steel magnate Lakshmi Mittal is the richest man in Britain, followed by Roman Abramovich with £10.8 billion.

Luxembourg has the highest minimum monthly wage in the world of £1,002. Romania's is £49.

The world's wealthiest university, Harvard University in Massachusetts, has a bigger budget than 142 countries, including Cuba, Jordan and Lithuania.

The poorer half of the world's population own barely 1% of global wealth.

Economists predicted that the World Cup in 2006 generated £900 million for the British economy solely through sales of barbeque food, snacks and beer.

The difference in prize money between finishing 4th and 5th in the Premiership is a staggering £26.5m. The difference between finishing 5th and 6th is just £2.6m.

Grey Goose vodka creator Sidney Frank bought a $400,000 black 2004 Mercedes Maybach and paid an extra $100,000 to make it bulletproof. The cushy ride features reclinable airline-style seats. The booze billionaire flies the car back and forth between his New York and San Diego homes. He also uses it to travel to golf courses, where he pays a team of pro golfers to play for his amusement.

News Corp chief Rupert Murdoch paid $44 million for a triplex on Manhattan's Fifth Avenue in December, setting a record for the amount paid for a city apartment.

It costs £39 to be a member of the Labour party, but only £15 to become a signed-up Conservative and £6 to join the Liberal Democrats.

In March 2006, Amanda Newkirk, a 7-month pregnant, 19 year-old waitress in Virginia, was left $1,000 to cover a $26.35 with a note saying 'Keep the change! Have a great day'.

The most expensive city in Britain to buy heroin and coaine is Belfast (£100 and £55 per gram respectively)

In 2006 454,000 Britons did all their Christmas shopping on Christmas Eve.

SALT WAS USED AS A CURRENCY IN PRE-COINAGE EUROPE.

CASH IN NUMBERS

£127,335 – Tony Blair's basic salary in 2006.

47 million Euro – the commercial worth of Ronaldinho to Barcelona, making him the most valuable football player 'brand' in the world.

$25 million – reward still on the head of Osama bin Laden from the FBI.

40% – amount of the world's wealth is owned by the richest 2% of the world's population.

260 – billionaires in the United States. Japan is second, way down on 29.

$1,547,620 – cost of the Mercedes Benz CLK/LM when launched. It remains the most expensive production car ever released.

£23,933 – the average cost to keep a British prisoner incarcerated for one year.

50 – percentage of bank robberies take place on Friday.

Five Need-to-know Nuggets About The Cost of the War in Iraq

1. Joseph Stiglitz, former chief economist of the World Bank and winner of the Nobel Prize for Economics, says the total costs of the Iraq War on the US economy will be between $1 trillion and $2 trillion.
2. As of March 2006, £4.5 billion had been spent by the UK in Iraq, all from a Government fund called the "Special Reserve" which has a current allocation of £6.44 billion.
3. About $2 billion worth of military equipment is wearing out or being destroyed every month in Iraq and Afghanistan. American charities such as Bake Sales For Body Armour, Soldiers' Angels and Operation Helment (a favourite of Cher) have sprung up to provide replacement gear.
4. The current US budget for the Iraq War includes $2.5 billion to combat roadside bombs and other improvised explosive devices, and $2.7 billion for intelligence activities.
5. The war costs American taxpayers $195,000 per day. One day in Iraq could feed all of the starving children in the world today almost four and a half times over.

***X Men 3: The Last Stand* remains the most expensive film ever released, with production costs reaching $210 million, just pipping *King Kong*'s $207 million.**

007 Daniel Craig's middle name is Wroughton.

Jack Black's parents were both rocket scientists.

Hugh Jackman wasn't supposed to be Wolverine in the* X-Men *films. He was a last-minute addition when Brit actor Dougray Scott dropped out.

Top Ten Pub Facts About, er, Pubs

1 Beer remains Britain's favourite alcoholic drink, accounting for 43% of pub sales.

2 Punch Taverns plc is the largest pub and bar operator in the United Kingdom, with 9,500 tenanted and managed pubs out of the total 61,000.

3 34% of couples met or had their first date in a pub.

4 Approximately a fifth of pubs and bars shut by eleven o'clock at the latest, and roughly half by midnight.

5 US President George W. Bush fulfilled his ambition of visiting a 'genuine English pub' during his November 2003 state visit to the UK when he had lunch and a pint of non-alcoholic lager with Tony Blair at the Dun Cow in Sedgefield, County Durham.

6 Pubs with 'Crown' in their title are the most popular in the United Kingdom, followed by those with 'Red Lion' and 'Royal Oak'.

7 Early pubs became so commonplace that in 965, King Edgar decreed that there should be no more than one alehouse per village. In 1393, King Richard II compelled landlords to erect signs outside their premises. The legislation stated "Whosoever shall brew ale in the town with intention of selling it must hang out a sign, otherwise he shall forfeit his ale."

8 Ball's Pond Road in Islington, London was named after a pub run by Mr Ball that had a pond to the rear of the premises filled with ducks. For a small fee, drinkers could go out and take their chance at shooting the fowl.

9 Outside Ireland, Germany has more Irish pubs than any other country. In 1995, Guinness opened 85 new pubs in Germany – the same number of new McDonald's outlets.

10 JD Wetherspoon isn't a real person. The name 'Wetherspoon' was one of founder Tim Martin's teachers, who once wrote in his school report that Martin would amount to nothing. The JD part came from Uncle Jesse Duke from *The Dukes of Hazzard*, one of Martin's favourite TV shows.

CLINT EASTWOOD ONCE BEAT UP FOUR SAILORS IN A BAR FOR "HAVING BAD MANNERS."

Brad Pitt is a trained journalist who dropped out towards the end of his Missouri University degree to pursue acting.

Simon Pegg is the godfather of Chris Martin and Gwyneth Paltrow's daughter Apple.

Matt Damon was originally down to play Daredevil *but the role eventually went to his real-life best friend Ben Affleck.*

In the Bond film *View To A Kill*, one of Christopher Walken's KGB bodyguards is Dolph Lundgren.

1995 Geena Davis-vehicle *Cutthroat Island* cost $100 million to produce and promote but earned back only $11 million – making it the biggest-ever box-office loser.

Tom Cruise makes a cameo in Young Guns, *but you have to look closely. After dropping by on set, the director agreed he could make an appearance, but only if he wore a really big moustache.*

In *Back To The Future*, when Michael J Fox visits Doc Brown's house, one of the clocks hanging on the wall has a clock featuring a little man hanging off one of the hands. This directly references the end of the film.

In The Big Lebowski, *you don't see The Dude bowl at any point during the film.*

Sylvester Stallone and Arnold Schwarzenegger were supposed to be the actors who had their faces switched in the eventual Nicholas Cage/John Travolta film *Face/ Off*.

In *Die Hard*, the Nakatomi building where Bruce Willis kicks arse in actually 20th Century Fox's head office.

One of the ninja-style guards Bruce Lee fights – and then puts in a headlock – in* Enter The Dragon *is none other than Jackie Chan.

Harrison Ford's second wife Melissa Mathison wrote the screenplay for ET.

The school in *Ferris Bueller's Day Off* is the same one used in *The Breakfast Club*.

Ed Norton's character in *Fight Club* doesn't have a name.

The lumberjack who gets his arm ripped out of its socket arm-wrestling Jeff Goldblum in The Fly is George Chuvalo, who fought Muhammad Ali for the world heavyweight title in 1966.

***Ghostbusters'* food-scoffing phantom Slimer was actually called Onionhead. It wasn't until the cartoon came out that his name was changed to Slimer.**

In *The Godfather*, the horse head that film boss Jack Waltz finds in his bed was real. The crew found the horse in a New Jersey rendering plant and had its head packed in ice and shipped to the set.

In Halloween, *serial killer Michael Myers wears a mask of Captain Kirk that's been painted white.*

In *Kill Bill: Volume I*, Uma Thurman drives past a wall featuring a "Red Apples" cigarette ad. "Red Apples" are a fictional brand that Quentin Tarantino uses in all his films.

In *Lord of the Rings: The Fellowship of the Ring*, you can see a car in the distant background as Frodo leaves his home in the shire.

In *The Passion of the Christ*, the hand that nails Jesus to the cross is Mel Gibson's.

At the end of Rocky V, *The Italian Stallion was supposed to die in Adrian's arms after being beaten to death by "Tommy Gunn" but the producers thought it was too downbeat.*

FILM IN NUMBERS

$100 million – Bruce Willis's fee for *The Sixth Sense*, the highest salary for an actor of all time.

91 – times police were called on Sacha Baron Cohen during the filming of *Borat*.

10 – Leonardo DiCaprio's age when his agent suggested he change his name to the more American-friendly Lenny Williams. DiCaprio declined.

$20million – The amount of dollars Robert De Niro was paid to appear in the 2005 Ben Stiller comedy *Meet The Fockers*.

6 – Words used by producers to pitch *Talladega Nights* to the studio: "Will Ferrell as a NASCAR driver".

4 – months added to the making of Mel Gibson's *Apocalypto* after torrential rains in Mexico brought the production to a stand-still.

9 – Cast and crew members died during the making of *The Exorcist*.

16 – Lines Arnie has in the first *Terminator* film.

237 – Number of both Red's prison cell in *The Shawshank Redemption* and the hotel room Jack Nicholson is forbidden to enter in *The Shining*. Stephen King wrote the stories both films were based on.

In the opening minutes of *Saving Private Ryan*, the soldiers who have their limbs blown off are real amputees. Spielberg did this to make his film more realistic.

The average person only feels 'adult' when they hit the age of 24, according to psychological studies.

Now-divorced Kid Rock and Pamela Anderson read their wedding vows to each other off their Blackberries.

Brazil is named after the nut, not the other way round.

Nobody know for sure why penguins are called penguins. It might be from the Latin pinguis, *meaning fat, or from the Welsh* pen gwyn' *meaning white head.*

Merry Clayton, who sang backing vocals on "Gimme Shelter" by The Rolling Stones, suffered a miscarriage due to the intensity of her performance.

Every US President with a beard has been a Republican.

According to English law, all males under 14 have to do two hours of longbow practice per week supervised by a local clergyman.

James is the most common name for a criminal.

Humans have four nostrils. We have two internal nostrils called choannae.

***TIME MAGAZINE*'S 'MAN OF THE YEAR' IN 1938 WAS ADOLF HITLER.**

Men spend approximately two years of their life in the toilet.

The highest mountain in the solar system is on Mars. Mount Olympus is 14 miles high and 388 miles across, almost three times the size of Mount Everest.

The Eiffel Tower grows seven inches in the summer.

Dave, of legendary cockney-knees-up duo Chas and Dave, is not a cockney.

The only band member without a beard in ZZ Top is called Frank Beard.

The dot over the letter 'i' is called a tittle.

The Swiss are the only European nation who eat dogs.

ELVIS PRESLEY'S MANAGER, COLONEL TOM PARKER, COVERED ALL BASES BY SELLING 'I HATE ELVIS' BADGES AS WELL AS 'I LOVE ELVIS' ONES.

The moon smells like gunpowder.

Entourage star Jeremy Piven's Range Rover has the personalised number plate PIVWEELZ.

People with an IQ of 140-plus are more likely to be left-handed than right-handed, despite lefties only making up 12% of the population.

2006 was the hottest year since records began in 1659.

SEX IN NUMBERS

1 in 7 priests and nuns break their vows of chastity.

14% of males did not enjoy sex the first time, compared to 60 per cent of women.

10.6 inches size of world's longest surgically-augmented penis, according to the Guinness Book Of Records.

80% of men who admit to climaxing while dreaming about sex, double the figure for women.

138 average shags a year for the Greeks, topping the global figures. They're followed by Croatians (134). Japanese are the least active on just 45 per year.

28mph speed of average man's initial spurt of ejaculate – faster than the world record for the 100 metre sprint.

1% of the adult female population are able to achieve orgasm solely through breast stimulation.

3 in 10 women over the age of 80 still have sexual intercourse.

112 calories burned by average female orgasm. A faked orgasm burns 315.

200 million couples around the world who have sex per day – or about 2,000 shags happening at any given moment.

IN THE AZTEC CULTURE, AVOCADOS WERE CONSIDERED SO SEXUALLY POWERFUL, VIRGINS WERE RESTRICTED FROM CONTACT WITH THEM.

Ecouteurism is listening to others having sex without their consent.

According to a recent survey, more Americans lose their virginity in June than any other month.

Hybristophilia is the arousal derived by having sex with criminals.

In America for three years during the 1950s, a campaign against 'naked animals' attracted considerable public support. Until, that is, the founders of the movement, Mr Trout and Mr Able, were exposed as inspired hoaxers.

In Pompeii, prostitutes had to dye their hair blue, red or yellow.

An analysis of speed-dating sessions across Britain found that every inch (2.5cm) a man has over a rival in height boosts his appeal to women by 5 per cent.

Impotence is grounds for divorce in 26 US states.

As a tranquilizer in the world, sex is ten times more effective than valium.

Worldwide averages show that Jews and atheists have more sex partners than Catholics or Protestants.

Besides the genitals and the breasts, the inner nose is the only other body part that swells during intercourse.

Australia has the planet's highest use of vibrators per head of population.

According to* Playboy*, more women talk dirty during sex than men.

Until 1972 in the US, homosexuality was officially a mental illness, classified with schizophrenia.

For every 35 pounds of weight a man carries over his ideal weight, his penis will appear to be one inch smaller.

In Florida and Washington DC, only the missionary position is legal.

Women with a PhD are TWICE as likely to be up for a one-night stand than those with a regular degree.

The Romans would crush a first-time rapist's gonads between two stones.

On Pacific island Guam, it is forbidden for virgins to marry, so there are men in Guam whose full-time job is to travel the country and deflower young women.

It takes a sperm one hour to swim seven inches.

If straight women had to choose a same-sex partner, a 2006 survey found that the most popular celebrity choice would by Davina McCall, followed by Jennifer Aniston and Kylie. Angelina Jolie surprisingly only collected 9% of the vote, lower than Zoe Ball.

Japan leads the world in condom use. Like cosmetics, they're sold door to door, by women.

The word pornography comes from the Greek meaning the "writings of prostitutes".

Of people who die suddenly during sex, eight in ten are in the act of cheating on their spouses.

Men are most likely to have affairs in the month of December, while women prefer July.

There is a town in Canada called Dildo.

The most common place for adults to have sex outside the bedroom is in the car, followed by toilets and the park.

The word 'vanilla' comes from the Latin word vagina, because of the pod's resemblance to the female genitalia.

A man's testicles can increase in size by 50 per cent when he is aroused.

Semen is the most common body fluid found in hotel rooms.

Five Need-to-know Nuggets About Pornography

1. *The Thais use pornography more than any other country.*
2. *40 per cent of British men in the UK admit to using pornographic websites in 2006.*
3. *Women are the fastest-growing users of pornography on the internet, with a 30 per cent rise in 2006.*
4. *Each year, in Los Angeles alone, more than 10,000 hardcore pornographic films are made, against an annual Hollywood average of just 400 movies.*
5. *Porn revenue is bigger than all combined revenues of all the professional football, baseball, and basketball franchises.*

ROUND BRITAIN BY FACT!

By law, all black London taxis must carry a bale of hay and a sack of oats.

Women in Bangor have been voted the ugliest in Britain. The North Wales city beat Gloucester, Exeter, Belfast, Plymouth, Glasgow and Hull to the title.

Norwich is the most badly behaved city in Britain, according to the ratio of population to minor misdemeanour.

There is a Yorkshire rose in the middle of the 20p coin.

Of all the world's cities, the word 'porn' is most frequently searched for in Birmingham. Manchester is 2nd and Brentford 8th.

Hull is the most stupid place in Britain, according to a combination of exam results, numbers of locals with degrees and performance in BBC IQ quiz Test the Nation.

TV chef Jean-Christophe Novelli liked his meal at Hemel Hampstead's Restaurant 65 so much last summer, he left a £900 tip.

There is only one registered sperm donor in Oxfordshire, making it the UK region that's officially meanest with jizz.

London has Euro's highest human-to-rat ratio, with 9 million rats to only 7 million humans. You're never more than 10 metres from a rat in the capital.

Amy Winehouse went to Croydon's Brits school – which has also given us Katie Melua, the Kooks and The Feeling.

Sunderland is the most sexually frustrated city in Britain, with eight out of ten people saying they're dissatisfied with the sex they're getting.

Bradford is the sexiest city in the UK, with 23% of residents claiming they shag daily.

There were 132 'big cat' sightings in Devon in 2006, the most in the United Kingdom.

Portsmouth is the rape capital of the UK, closely followed by Peterborough.

There are more speed cameras in Mid and South Wales (377) than any other region in the UK. The lowest is Hertfordshire with only 31.

The first official international football match was played at the West of Scotland Cricket Club in Partick in 1872, between Scotland and England.

There are more pubs and bars per square mile in Nottingham than in any other European city.

SPORT'S EXTREME BODY PARTS

NECK

England prop Andrew Sheridan has some fairly impressive stats – the 215kg he benchpresses means he could qualify for GB's Olympic weight-lifting team – but it's all based on the power that comes from the 8.5-inch-thick wedge of muscle he disguises as a neck. The average male collar size is 16in. Sheridan has shirts specially made with a 21in collar.

HEART

Miguel Indurain won five consecutive Tour de Frances in the nineties – partly because his heart was 50 per cent bigger than most people's. His resting heart rate of 28–29 beats per minute meant he was almost clinically dead (yours is about 70 bpm).

ELBOW

The combination of a naturally crooked elbow (it's 32 degrees away from the norm) and a double-jointed wrist means Sri Lankan wizard Muttiah Muralitharan can spin the ball unlike anyone else (Warne included). It's brought him 674 Test wickets and so much controversy that he was forced to bowl in a metal brace in 2004 to prove he doesn't chuck the ball.

HAND

His height (7ft 2ins) and weight (24st) probably help, but it's with his massive fists that Nikolai Valuev has battered his way to the world heavyweight title. Held next to each other, his clenched fists measure a whole foot across, making them literally twice as big as yours.

THIGHS

The reason Real Madrid and Brazil full-back Roberto Carlos (occasionally) hits free-kicks at face-threatening speed? His absurdly large thighs. They're 24 inches in diameter, the same size as Muhammad Ali's when he was heavyweight champ. Pretty impressive when you consider that Ali was nine inches and five stone bigger than Carlos.

FEET

With 22 world records, Aussie swimmer Ian 'Thorpedo' Thorpe is the closest thing to a fish that the human race has ever produced. The biggest similarity to sea life? His over-sized flippers – otherwise known as size 17 feet.

SPORT IN NUMBERS

15 – Age of Peter Simple, the oldest horse to win the Grand National back in 1853. The oldest jockey was Dick Saunders who was 48 when he rode Grittar to victory in 1982.

2.3 – Average goals per game at the 2006 World Cup

40 mph – Speed of a dart travelling to the board.

213 – Aces served by Goran Ivanisevic on his way to the 2001 Wimbledon crown.

£400 million – Value of balls used by golfers each year.

55 – Seconds Michael Owen and Wayne Rooney, England's first-choice strike partnership, played together at the 2006 World Cup.

7.6 – Miles surfed by Steve King to set a new world record recently.

100 million – Worldwide TV viewers who watched recent Ladbrokes World Championship Darts Final between Raymond Barneveld and Phil Taylor.

0.25 per cent – growth in German economy attributable to the World Cup.

2 – Grey horses to win the Grand National. The Lamb won it in 1868 and 1871 and Nicholaus Silver won it in 1961.

7 – Seconds it took for Freddie Eastwood to score on his Southend debut.

0 – Goals conceded by Switzerland in being knocked out of the 2006 World Cup.

The first foreigner to win England's Footballer of the Year was Manchester City's German goalkeeper Bert Trautmann in 1956 – he once famously played on after breaking his neck. The next was another German, Jurgen Klinsman, almost 40 years later in 1995.

Until 1967, it wasn't illegal for Olympic athletes to use drugs to enhance their performance during competition.

Mary Queen of Scots, the first known female golfer, coined the term "caddy" in 1552, calling her assistants cadets. During her reign, the famous golf course at St. Andrews was built.

Tim Henman's great grandmother Ellen Mary Stawell-Brown was, in 1901, the first woman to use an overarm serve at Wimbledon.

WEST BROMWICH ALBION PLAY AT THE HIGHEST ALTITUDE IN THE ENGLISH LEAGUE, AT 551 FT ABOVE SEA LEVEL.

ANDREW STRAUSS HAS WON 75 PER CENT OF TEST MATCHES HE HAS CAPTAINED – THE MOST BY ANY SKIPPER UNDER COACH DUNCAN FLETCHER.

A total of 22 players scored in the penalty shoot-out between Ivory Coast and Cameroon at the African Cup Of Nations 2005, a record in international football; Ivory Coast won 12–11.

MICHAEL ESSIEN PLAYED 2,160 MINUTES PLAYED THIS SEASON UP UNTIL CHRISTMAS, THE MOST BY ANY PLAYER IN THE PREMIERSHIP.

It was 63 Grands Prix without a British winner until August 2006. David Coulthard won in Australia in 2003, the next British winner was Jenson Button in Hungary.

Two Juventus youth team players recently died after trying to retrieve a ball from a lake at the club's Turin training ground.

The 167 runs hit off Shane Warne in the second 2007 ashes test is the highest amount he's ever conceded in an innings.

The longest match played in Wimbledon's history lasted 369 minutes, as Mark Knowles and Daniel Nestor beat Simon Aspelin and Todd Perry 5–7, 6–3, 6–7, 6–3, 23–21 in the men's doubles.

Mike Hussey's average in Test cricket, prior to the Fourth Ashes Test, was 86.33 – the second highest in history, behind Aussie legend Donald Bradman's 99.

LUOL DENG, THE BRIXTON-RAISED CHICAGO BULLS BASKETBALL STAR – AND BRITAIN'S HIGHEST-PAID SPORTSMAN – IS THE SON OF A FORMER DEPUTY PRIME MINISTER OF SUDAN.

Ryan Giggs was the first player to win back-to-back PFA Young Player of the Year awards in 1992 and 1993.

The lowest points total won by Premiership winners came in 1997 when Man United took the crown with just 75 points. That would have secured third place in 2007.

The smallest ever FA Cup-winning captain was Sunderland's 1973 skipper Bobby Kerr who was a diminutive 5ft 4ins.

The highest break (68) in the 2006 Snooker World Championship Final, made by winner Graeme Dott, was the lowest in finals history.

An unnamed bidder paid £26,400 for the ball hit by West Indies legend Garry Sobers for six sixes in an over.

£12m was paid to buy horse "The Green Monkey", a world-record price. The stud has not raced and is no longer in training.

Retired Australian cricketer Justin Langer has black belts in Tai kwon do and Zen do kai.

Roger Federer only served five double faults in winning Wimbledon in 2006.

Micah Richards is only the second player with the initials MR to represent England. The first was Michael Ricketts.

Five Need-to-know Nuggets About Barcelona

1. *Futbol Club Barcelona were formed in 1899 by a group of Swiss, Catalan and English men.*
2. *They now have 151,000 members, who effectively own the club. There are 1,782 recognised Barça fanclubs throughout the world.*
3. *The fans are nicknamed* Culés, *which translates into "arses". It's not an insult – in the early days, the backsides of the top row of fans could be seen from outside the ground.*
4. *Barcelona claim to have won 106 trophies in the club's history, including 18 Spanish League titles and two European Cups. But they recently lost the World Club Championship Final to Independiente of Argentina.*
5. *Barcelona finally took a shirt sponsor in 2006, donating £1m a year to children's charity UNICEF to carry their logo. They had refused shirts sponsors previously to that.*

GET YOUR DAILY SLICE OF ZOO!

The very best of ZOO, including the sexiest real girls, the latest sporting news and the funniest celeb stories – all on the web!

Meet 100s of hot real girl bloggers

Watch exclusive scorching hot girls on film

Be first for the best viral videos

Get daily breaking news from man-world

See star babes showing skin

Log on to

zooweekly.co.uk

for your daily dose of the best from the blokesphere

ZOO contains the best girls, the best sport and the best news every week.

ZOO

Free UK delivery!

Subscribe Now!

Get your copy delivered direct to your door for only £15 by quarterly Direct Debit*... That's a saving of over £11 off a year's subscription and you don't have to fight the queue in your newsagents to get your copy every week. What more could you ask for?!

Visit www.greatmagazines.co.uk/zoo or call: 0845 126 3333 quoting DQCC.

*Minimum subscription term is 12 months, UK offer only.

*Small print: Direct debit offer – minimum subscription term is 12 months. Calls from BT landlines will be charged at 4p per minute at all times, mobile phone tariffs vary. UK offer only – for overseas offers visit www.greatmagazines.co.uk